jogging

by

WILLIAM J. BOWERMAN
Professor of Physical Education
Track Coach
University of Oregon

and

W. E. HARRIS, M.D.

with

JAMES M. SHEA
University of Oregon

Published in Association with *This Week Magazine*

Publishers GROSSET & DUNLAP *New York*

Library of Congress Catalog Card Number: 67-16154

Published simultaneously in Canada.

Printed in the United States of America

INTRODUCTION

As with most good ideas, jogging began in many places. It has some of the flavor of scientific findings that are announced simultaneously by different discoverers.

No one knows who was the first jogger. Maybe it was one of the Greeks. They were fond of physical exercise, particularly running.

In this country and elsewhere, hardy independent men and women have jogged for years, their natural instincts providing just the right personal exercise program. Physicians, coaches, physical education instructors have long preached the value of exercise and outlined the potentialities of different kinds of exercise, including running.

In New Zealand, thanks to the work of Arthur Lydiard, the New Zealand Olympic coach, jogging is almost a way of life. Lydiard developed his version of jogging for some of his runners who were about to retire from competition and who were unwilling to give up the high level of fitness built through training.

Lydiard came up with the idea of combining conditioning with the stimulus of companionship by slow steady cross-country running done in loosely organized groups or jogging "clubs." The active citizenry took to it in a big way. Whole communities, from toddler to grandma, jog on weekends and holidays.

In 1962 Bill Bowerman, who in the past 20 years has trained some of the world's most successful runners, toured New Zealand with the University of Oregon's world record four-mile relay team. He found not only good competition for his runners, but a citizenry with great zest for physical activity, possessed of the same vigor that characterized Americans 50 years ago. The vitality of the "over 30" was particularly impressive. Compared to New Zealanders, the level of fitness here for a person over 30 was inadequate.

In fact, Bowerman found his own fitness inadequate. One afternoon, at 50 and fit, or so he thought, he joined Lydiard and the two teams for an easy workout over the New Zealand countryside. Quickly he was alone. Running easily and without a puff, the others glided away and out of sight. Following that experience, Bowerman began to jog regularly. In two weeks, his fitness improved, he confidently set out for a jog with a group of about 200 men, women and children. After a half mile, h was alone again. Only a 76-year-old man was nearby. As th two jogged, the old gentleman's presence became painful to a already bruised ego; the old fellow was being courteous, hold ing himself back and waiting for Bowerman.

The New Zealand experience impressed Bowerman deeply When he returned home, he continued to jog. He also talked t the press who listened because he was one of the country's mos successful track coaches.

Shortly, Bowerman unwittingly found himself the leader o something amounting to a cause. Thousands of people, out o shape and uncertain what to do about it, heard of jogging an wanted details. They phoned, wrote and stopped by in person

Meanwhile, Bowerman jogged and speculated: in his year of coaching he had evolved basic conditioning principles tha regularly brought his runners to a high level of fitness. Wh couldn't the same principles, in scaled-down versions, be applie to train typical businessmen and housewives in poor physica condition from lack of exercise?

To test the idea, Bowerman was joined by Dr. W. E. Harris a cardiologist, who was interested in the concept that regula exercise might be an important factor in preventing certain type of heart disease. The two conducted a number of "controlled study programs with adults aged 25 to 66. Word of the pro grams and the preliminary results spread quickly. Other group applied the Bowerman and Harris principles, and many commu nities started jogging programs. Today, there are thousands o contented joggers, all much more fit than before they bega jogging.

This book is about "why's" and "how to's" of jogging. It wi show how you, too, can enjoy life more fully through bette fitness and health.

James M. Shea
Eugene, Oregon
February, 1967

AUTHORS' NOTE

fter talking, advising and lecturing about jogging for so long, is a relief at last to write about it.

We are interested in exercise, and especially jogging, for ·veral reasons. First, it's generally accepted that moderate regu-r exercise benefits health. Unfortunately, a large number of merican men and women over 30 do not exercise regularly, ıd in fact, lead sedentary lives.

Second, there are drawbacks to many of the available physi-ıl activities and sports. These shortcomings include: expense, ›nvenience, time involved, availability of facilities, required :ills and the regularity of participation. Other activities pro-de little actual exercise, or the exercise is intermittent, with ·st being taken as soon as the person is a little tired or breath-ss. The result—little stress placed on the body to improve ıysical fitness, especially of the cardiovascular and respiratory 'stems.

Jogging, by contrast, has special advantages for adults. First, 's simple, requires no extensive skills, is convenient and in-›lves a minimum of time each week.

Second, it is an excellent exercise from a physiological point view because it places the moderate stress on the cardio-ıscular system and respiratory system so important to general ·alth.

The third point—and the reason jogging is different—is that alternates running and walking. This makes it possible to con-›l the degree of exertion by controlling the distance, speed running and amount of walking.

To summarize: jogging is a graduated program of moderate ercise which can be adapted to men and women of varying ;es and levels of fitness.

A few final words: Jogging is a simple type of exercise, re-ıiring no highly developed skills. Its great appeal is that it so handy. Almost anyone can do it anywhere. Our concern to keep it simple, not let it become hidden in some mystique ll of rules and paraphernalia.

William J. Bowerman
W. E. Harris, M.D.

CAUTION

Experience shows that most people can follow the moderate, gradually increasing exercise of the jogging training program without difficulties.

Nevertheless, anyone jogging without medical supervision should consult a physician promptly if any unusual symptoms develop.

OVER 30 OR WELL OVER 30? RELAX, AND HAVE A MEDICAL CHECK-UP

The jogging training program can benefit all age levels. However, if you are over 30, or well over 30, and haven't been exercising *regularly,* begin your program relaxed and in the best frame of mind by having a preliminary medical examination. As you age, the incidence of certain diseases is higher—particularly diseases of the heart and lungs. A preliminary medical examination sometimes reveals previously unrecognized disabilities (see page 16 for further discussion).

YOUR MEDICAL HISTORY AND EXERCISE PROGRAMS

Any form of exercise may be harmful if your medical history includes problems of the heart, lungs or joints. When such conditions exist, consult your physician before entering any exercise program.

1

This book is about jogging, an exercise program of relaxed walking and running that will improve the level of physical fitness of nearly anyone from seven to 70.

There is nothing mysterious or revolutionary about it. Jogging is simply a unique application of the accepted principle that regular exercise in moderate amounts is good for most people.

Jogging is free. It is convenient and enjoyable. It is safe. It requires no special skills or equipment. And it can benefit nearly everyone who is not ill or disabled. At the same time, it has special benefits for the "over 30" and the "well over 30" groups who no longer *regularly* exercise. Through jogging they can recapture a level of physical fitness they thought they had lost forever.

And jogging is reasonable. You can grow fit without greatly changing your personal habits. Within reason, you can still eat what you like . . . take a drink. Remember only that good sense is the best guide to healthful living.

JOGGING IS DIFFERENT

Jogging is different from most popular physical fitness programs.

Unlike weight lifting, isometric exercises and calisthenics with their emphasis on muscle building, jogging works to improve the heart, lungs, and circulatory system. Other body muscles are exercised as well, but the great benefit comes from improving the way the heart and lungs work.

After all, when you're past 30, bulging biceps and pleasing pectorals may boost your ego, *but your life and health may depend upon how fit your heart and lungs are.*

WHY COMBINE WALKING AND RUNNING?

Jogging as a form of exercise has the advantage of alternate walking and running. Both walking and running are good exercises. Each has its advocates. Done separately, each may fall a bit short of what is needed—gradually increased stress on the heart and lungs. For the fit, walking may not be strenuous enough. For the average person, running may be too strenuous at the start.

By combining running and walking, nearly anyone can begin to jog safely and comfortably. The amount of exercise can be gradually increased. *You do not accidentally overexert yourself.* By gradually increasing the amount of running and pace, you eventually can train yourself to a level that will . . . well, astound you.

Remember, regular exercise should be part of a long-range health program. The benefits are short-lived if you exercise only for a few months.

THREE DEFINITIONS OF JOGGING

Before going further, it might be helpful to look again at the term, jogging. Actually, it can be used three ways: (1) Jogging means a steady or an easy-paced run alternating with breath catching periods of walking; (2) it means a kind of running, generally a slow regular trot that has been described as the next step up from walking; and (3) it is a word that describes the entire program of physical fitness outlined in this book.

THE UNIQUE APPLICATION

The jogging program in this book is based on medical observation, proven training principles and, equally important, the experience of other joggers.

Earlier, jogging was described as a *unique* application of the accepted principle that regular exercise in moderate amounts is good for most people. Many people have run for this reason but have had to rely on their own instincts to provide the right program. Now, for the first time, the training principles have been articulated, medical advice applied, and these factors organized into three usable plans complete with schedules.

SCHEDULES ARE THE HEART OF JOGGING

These schedules are the heart of the jogging program. They tell you how far, how fast and how often to jog. They leave little to chance. The schedules assume that, unlike the runner, you may have to be your own coach and trainer. So everything is spelled out for you. *If you follow the instructions, you do not overwork.*

WHY SCHEDULES?

The jogging program is based on experience in the conditioning of runners and joggers. It uses schedules throughout the training period to establish a *permanent habit* of regular moderate exercise. So keep in mind as you begin that even world class runners train as you do by repeated practice of certain exercises.

With the coach they schedule certain exercises to get specific results. For example, different exercises might be designed to improve the runner's skill on the track, enlarge his lung capacity, affect general physical conditioning, and control breathing. Joggers' and runners' exercises are not based on whim or chance. They are the product of careful thought and scientific knowledge. There are good and sound reasons for how an exercise is performed, its duration and the number of times it is repeated.

It is beyond the scope of this book and probably beyond your interest to describe the physiological changes in runners through training. After all, you are primarily interested in how training will change your life and improve your health.

2
PRACTICAL ADVANTAGES OF JOGGING

Most men and women who are out of shape know it. They have a guilty feeling that they really ought to be doing something about it. What's lacking is the opportunity. The ease of taking up jogging solves that problem. Consider jogging's special, practical advantages:

IT'S FREE: Not a thing about jogging costs you a cent. True, you may have to spend some will power to start. That shouldn't bankrupt you. The chances are great for a wealth of good health.

NO SPECIAL EQUIPMENT: You, yourself, are the only equipment necessary. Many fitness programs cost a great deal before the first workout. Not so with jogging. Ladies with only high heels will need a pair of flats.

NO SPECIAL FACILITIES: No gymnasium, barbells, pool, or muscle building gimmicks. Just open your door and you're in business. Jog anywhere, outside or indoors.

QUICK: There are 1,440 minutes in a day. For beginners, jogging takes about 30 minutes three days a week, or only 90 minutes out of 10,080 each week. If you're over 30 and unwilling to spend this minimum time for better fitness, you'd better be prepared to spend even more time being ill.

OLD AND YOUNG CAN DO IT: Anyone from seven to 70, not ill or disabled, can benefit from jogging's gradual moderate exercise. Thousands of joggers are proving this every day.

IT'S ENJOYABLE; IT'S FUN: People enjoy little things that bring big rewards. Jogging makes few demands. Usually progress is steady. You can enjoy the feeling of accomplishment.

WHAT'S IN IT FOR YOU?

What's in it for you may add up to quite a bit, if you care about your life. Frankly, jogging may prolong your life.

Now, if you still question the merits of jogging, consider these advantages:

IT'S SAFE: Jogging exercises are gradual. If you follow the workout schedules, *you do not overexert*. Each jogging schedule starts at *your* level of fitness.

IMPROVES THE HEART AND LUNGS: The jogging exercises work at improving the heart, lungs, and circulatory system by gradually expanding their capacity to handle stress. Jogging conditions the rest of you too, but the benefit comes from the better way the heart and lungs work. Someday your life may depend upon their fitness.

YOU LOOK AND FEEL BETTER: Exercise stimulates circulation, tones the muscles and produces a more optimistic outlook. Jogging reduces the hips and thighs, firms sagging muscles and flattens the abdomen. Also, those who are in good condition are more active sexually. There is a psychological element as well. If you look and feel better, you gain confidence. You feel more attractive.

HELPS YOU LOSE WEIGHT: Jogging is an aid to losing weight. Through jogging you can reduce the amount of fat and increase the amount of muscle. Jogging plus diet will guarantee you good weight loss.

BUILDS ENDURANCE AND CONFIDENCE: Jogging makes you more fit. You can confidently tackle your job, increase your work load, or set out to enjoy recreational activity without fear of overexerting your heart. The fit jogger is not among the heart attack victims during hunting season.

SMALLER WAISTLINE: Jogging helps redistribute weight. In controlled programs nearly all joggers reduced the size of the waistline. Women dropped down in dress size.

JOG ALONE OR WITH OTHERS: If you crave time alone, then jog by yourself. You can think without distraction or just put your mind to sleep. If you like the company of others, group jogging provides great companionship.

A LIFETIME OF BETTER HEALTH: Exercise should be a part of a long-range health program. Regular exercise year in and year out is what counts. Short term exercise gets short term results. Jogging is so accessible you can hardly avoid it.

ESPECIALLY FOR THE LADIES

Society has made nearly everyone conscious of the need to exercise. Due in part to feminine fashions, women who are out of shape have an even guiltier feeling about it than men. Where men's traditional clothes camouflage flab, women's fashions expose the figure. Furthermore, fashion demands that every woman look young, no matter what her age.

What to do? There are exercises for women that are popular and socially acceptable; for example, calisthenics in a class or at home in front of the TV set. Golf, swimming, bowling, tennis and bicycle riding are others. They're all fun if you care for them, but each may have some shortcoming. One may not be the right kind of exercise for what you need; another may cost too much; others may be inconvenient as to hour or locale.

Jogging, on the other hand, has some extra special virtues that women should consider.

1. *Jogging improves the legs in many ways.*
   a. Jogging slims and firms them. Contrary to what some women think, jogging does not build heavy or bulky muscles. For evidence, look at runners. Traditionally they have long well-proportioned legs with the kinds of long extended muscles that add to good looks.
   b. Jogging builds the calf for skinny legs.
   c. Jogging trims the ankles.
   d. Some women joggers report a significant decrease in muscle cramps of the leg at night.
2. *Jogging slims the waistline:* Not everyone who jogs will lose weight. But jogging redistributes weight, and nearly everyone who jogs slims the waistline. Women who did not want to lose weight, kept their weight but still dropped down in dress size because the weight was redistributed.
3. *Jogging reduces the hips and flattens the abdomen:* Again look to runners for evidence. Characteristically they have slim hips and flat abdomens.
4. *Jogging firms sagging muscles:* Jogging works the entire body, developing the long muscles that contribute to good looks. Women joggers report a decrease in loose fat on the underside of the upper arm and under the chin.
5. *Jogging is thrifty:* Women, more then men, seem reluctant to part with money for schemes. They develop the habit of "making do." They rationalize that they can do it themselves, something like baking bread at home. Well, with jogging they can. Jogging is free.

3

EXERCISE AND HEALTH

For the sedentary adult, the most strenuous exercise may be a short walk to the bus stop or a stroll with the dog.

Yet, things haven't always been this way. Man has been physically active throughout his history. It is only in the 20th century that technological progress has permitted a large proportion of the population to work at jobs requiring little physical activity. With the decrease in physical activity has come an increase in diseases of the blood vessels and the heart. The Metropolitan Life Insurance Company reports that in 1966, diseases of the heart and arteries accounted for more than half of the deaths in the United States.

PHYSICAL ACTIVITY AND "HEART ATTACKS"

A "heart attack" (in medical terms, a myocardial infarction) is the single biggest killer in the United States. There is no known drug or single way to prevent it. Even if you survive an attack, you may suffer marked disability and limitation of activity. The myocardium is the heart muscle and a myocardial infarction is caused by a blockage of the blood that flows through the coronary arteries to supply the heart muscle. A common cause of the blockage of the blood flow is a clot, or "coronary thrombosis," that forms in a coronary artery.

Unquestionably, many factors are involved in causing heart attacks. Lack of physical exercise is only one. But medical research indicates it may be among the most important. Heredity is also a factor. Though the physiological weaknesses inherited from one's parents cannot be changed, they may be offset somewhat by a higher level of physical fitness.

Recent medical reports have found that the least active men had more myocardial infarctions, and more were fatal. The most active men not only had a lower incidence of attacks, but their chances of survival were considerably greater. Both the incidence and severity of an initial myocardial infarction were reduced in the most active as compared to the least active men.

Men who did little walking had almost twice the mortality rate of walkers. Men who rarely engage in sports also have nearly twice the mortality rate of more active men.

The reports suggest that a substantial reduction of deaths from myocardial infarctions might be achieved through a relatively small increase in physical activities of the inactive men in a given population.

It is believed that those who habitually are more physically active may develop a better blood supply to the heart muscle than those who are inactive.

From these reports it appears that regular exercise may be an important factor in reducing the risk of myocardial infarctions or "heart attacks" in men.

HEART ATTACKS IN MEN AND WOMEN

As a group, men have more heart attacks than women. Unless there is some predisposing cause such as diabetes or high blood pressure, heart attacks among women are uncommon before the menopause. After the menopause, women are affected at about the same frequency as men in their age groups.

There is practically no reliable data on the relationship between activity in women and the incidence of "heart attacks." Theoretically, increased physical activity would have the same beneficial effect as in men, but at a somewhat later time in life.

OVER 30 AND UNDERPRIVILEGED

From a health viewpoint, recent medical data suggests that exercise after 30 may be more important than activity performed earlier in life.

And yet, if you're over 30, you're underprivileged when it comes to real opportunities for physical exercise. You may not realize it, but you've been discriminated against by most of the professionals—coaches, teachers, athletic directors—who have unintentionally put you aside to work almost exclusively with the younger generation.

For example, go to a football stadium on any Saturday afternoon in the fall. There are 22 well-conditioned and well-fed players on the field, and another 80 or so along the sideline. With them is a staff of 14 to 20, including coaches, assistant coaches, trainers, equipment managers, and physicians. Each is keenly interested in the health and fitness of the players. Just standing around in their expensive equipment, the players represent a tremendous investment of time, money, and professional training.

Or, go to a Little League baseball final and marvel at the professional way the youngsters play. The field is a miniature major league diamond. The equipment and coaching techniques are modeled on the big leagues. In swimming, track and field, tennis, golf and other sports, the professionals have provided wondrous programs for the youngsters who take advantage of them.

Professionals unwittingly discriminate further in that they spend little time on the youngsters with small talent or with those who don't care to compete.

What happens to the same boys and girls when they finish high school and college and find themselves in the adult world? More often than not, they exercise less and add weight while sliding toward physical unfitness. Exercise is available but quite often requires special equipment and facilities. It may also be expensive and inconvenient. There is some question as to whether or not much of the physical activity is the right type or actually does much good for general health.

TYPICAL "AFTER-30" EXERCISES

One punster suggests that the principle exercises for some over 30 are: running down their friends, jumping to conclusions, side-stepping responsibility and pushing their luck. A more acceptable list is golf, bowling, hunting, isometric exercises, weight lifting, fishing, and calisthenics at home or at a health club.

Many of the best known conditioning programs go overboard on calisthenics and do not provide enough endurance exercises. However, for the "over 30," any moderate, regular exercise program has both physical and psychological advantages.

MEDICAL ADVICE IMPORTANT BEFORE ANY EXERCISE PROGRAM

Joggers from seven to 70 have found the jogging program an enjoyable way to pursue physical fitness. Nearly all participate without discomfort. Still, there are those who should *not* jog.

As part of the study leading to this book, "controlled" programs were conducted for adults "over 30." The number of participants was limited so that each participant received personal attention. The programs lasted 12 weeks. Each included 106 to 141 participants, aged 30 to 67. The exercises were the same as the exercises in this book; moderate, gradually increased walking and running exercises aimed at toning up the heart, lungs, and circulatory system.

Before admission to the controlled programs, applicants underwent a medical examination. About 15 per cent of the applicants had some disability of the heart or lungs that they were unaware of that merited medical supervision. Another two percent were advised not to jog at all. They had medical disorders that jogging or any type of vigorous exercise would have aggravated.

The fact that this group was unaware of such significant disabilities underscores the importance of medical advice before entering any exercise program.

A caution: Most joggers can follow the jogging training schedule with little difficulty other than the normal aches and pains. For some "over 30" and especially for the "well over 30" there may be potential dangers in unsupervised exercise. If you wish to jog by yourself, without first participating in a supervised jogging program, see your physician and get his permission.

EXERCISE CAN PRODUCE ACHES AND PAINS

Many aches and pains that develop while jogging are harmless. Any time you exercise beyond your normal level of activity or exceed your level of physical fitness, you can expect some soreness. Even the simplest exercises, when not done regularly, may produce discomfort. Getting into shape is a complicated physiological process. Muscles, ligaments and tendons must adjust to the new and increased stresses. Remember the sore knees and stiff muscles when you turned out for football after a lazy summer, or the sore calves following the first long ride on your bike in the spring? If you did more than usual, the next day you had tender muscles. These normal aches and pains corrected themselves as you kept exercising. As you grow older, normal aches and pains still correct themselves, but not so easily nor with the same speed.

NORMAL ACHES AND PAINS FOR THE "OVER 30"

Most joggers, particularly in the "over 30" group can expect some twinges and pains as they begin the program. Leg and back muscles, long retired, may ache after the first few workouts. This is normal. You don't notice the change while walking. However, at the first scheduled running, even though slow and for a short time, the muscles may balk at the load. If this happens, most should stick to the schedule and keep jogging. The stiffness and the aches should disappear as you grow more fit.

One common complaint among the "over 30" is the soreness that develops around old knee or ankle injuries or healed fractures. When such aches and pains occur, see the jogger's reconditioning program (page 37) for proper treatment.

If the discomfort is more than just mild or if it persists, consult your physician.

4
FOLKS WHO ARE FAT

If fat is too gross a term, will you settle for overweight? All right then, regardless of its causes, overweight is a major health problem in the United States. Insurance statistics show that overweight is associated with a high death rate. Diabetes, gall bladder disease, hypertension and heart disease are all more frequent in overweight persons. So if you are lugging around those extra pounds, prospects for a long life are not too bright.

WHO IS OVERWEIGHT?

At 10 per cent over your desirable weight, you are overweight. If you are 20 per cent above your desired weight, you are considered obese.

Got a full length mirror handy? Take a good look front and back. What's the conclusion? Be honest. Now check the Metropolitan Life Insurance Company weight tables shown here to see what your approximate weight should be. There are three body frames. Choose the right one and don't fudge. If in doubt, choose the smaller frame. A surprising number of joggers in the "controlled" study groups had normal weight.

If you need to shed some pounds, regular exercise can help. Overweight and lack of exercise are often related. If you are overweight you tend to exercise less, and lack of exercise tends to cause added weight.

Jogging is an excellent exercise to aid in losing weight. By walking and running, you consume calories at a rapid rate.

Losing weight depends on the balance between the energy you expend and the number of calories you take in through your diet. Other factors are rarely important. So if you increase your physical activity you may lose some weight. If you eat less and combine it with increased physical activity you guarantee a weight loss.

Remember, no matter how strenuously you exercise, there

DESIRABLE WEIGHTS FOR WOMEN 25 AND OVER*

(Weight According to Frame—In Indoor Clothing)

HEIGHT† feet inches	SMALL FRAME	MEDIUM FRAME	LARGE FRAME
4 10	92-98	96-107	104-119
4 11	94-101	98-110	106-122
5 0	96-104	101-113	109-125
5 1	99-107	104-116	112-128
5 2	102-110	107-119	115-131
5 3	105-113	110-122	118-134
5 4	108-116	113-126	121-138
5 5	111-119	116-130	125-142
5 6	114-123	120-135	129-146
5 7	118-127	124-139	133-150
5 8	122-131	128-143	137-154
5 9	126-135	132-147	141-158
5 10	130-140	136-151	145-163
5 11	134-144	140-155	149-168
6 0	138-148	144-159	153-173

† with shoes on—2-inch heels

DESIRABLE WEIGHTS FOR MEN 25 AND OVER*

(Weight According to Frame—In Indoor Clothing)

HEIGHT‡ feet inches	SMALL FRAME	MEDIUM FRAME	LARGE FRAME
5 2	112-120	118-129	126-141
5 3	115-123	121-133	129-144
5 4	118-126	124-136	132-148
5 5	121-129	127-139	135-152
5 6	124-133	130-143	138-156
5 7	128-137	134-147	142-161
5 8	132-141	138-152	147-166
5 9	136-145	142-156	151-170
5 10	140-150	146-160	155-174
5 11	144-154	150-165	159-179
6 0	148-158	154-170	164-184
6 1	152-162	158-175	168-189
6 2	156-167	162-180	173-194
6 3	160-171	167-185	178-199
6 4	164-175	172-190	182-204

‡ with shoes on—1-inch heels

* Data prepared by Metropolitan Life Insurance Company

aren't enough hours in the day to burn off the fat if you are already overweight and continue to overeat.

Do not use jogging as a license to stuff yourself.

If your weight problem is slight, chances are that exercise alone will take care of it.

GIRTH CONTROL

Almost without exception, joggers report a measurable decrease in waistlines after about six to eight weeks of faithful adherence to the schedule. Two to three inches is quite common.

Often, and for good reason, there is no comparable weight loss during the same period. The reason is that solid muscle weighs more than fat, but takes less space.

And while the waistline shrinks, the chest measurement expands, a natural result of using the lungs more fully and regularly. The redistribution of weight and bulk may be all you want or need to look as well as you feel.

NO CRASH DIETS OR FOOD FADS

Life is for enjoyment and crash diets tend to lessen the enjoyment. They have other disadvantages as well: (1) they often do not provide proper nutritional value, (2) they can't be followed permanently, (3) they're expensive, (4) they are boring and (5) in most cases the loss of weight is only temporary.

If you are serious about losing weight, the important principles are as follows:

(1) Reduce the daily calorie intake. In simpler language, eat less. The reason you are overweight is normally not glandular or hereditary; you just stay too long at the table. You will lose weight if you eat fewer calories than needed to maintain your present weight. The deficit of 500 calories a day, while maintaining the same level of physical activity, will result in a loss of about one pound per week. As a suggestion, try adding the "push away" to your jogging exercises. Three times a day practice pushing away from the table before you have a second helping. Continue to eat what you are accustomed to but in smaller amounts.

(2) Eat a properly balanced diet. Nutrition specialists recommend that an adequately balanced diet should include daily

ervings from: (a) the milk group, including cheese; (b) the neat group, including eggs, fish, poultry and nuts; (c) the fruit and vegetable group and (d) the bread and cereal group. Nurition specialists further recommend that the overall diet should be low in fat and carbohydrate, moderate in protein such as neats, and high in the relatively low-calorie fruits and vegetables.

(3) Exercise regularly and change your eating habits. Eating s largely a matter of habit and research shows that increased exercise unless it is carried on strenuously for a long period of ime does not increase your appetite. While you exercise you pend more calories. If you will just eat less, or the same amount, ou will steadily lose weight.

(4) Proper motivation—think thin. This may be the most difficult of the principles. The happy fat person is a myth. Normally he is miserable, ashamed of his appearance. If you re chronically overweight and really want to reduce, it takes great courage on your part and understanding from the rest of he family. Through exercise and diet, you will look and feel better.

THE HOUSEWIFE HAS SPECIAL PROBLEMS

Because meals are often hurried and the kitchen is always handy, he housewife has a special problem. She may eat continuously between meals rather than overeating at mealtime. The nibbling dds up to more than she realizes.

If finding enough time for more regular meals is impossible nd snacks are necessary, stick to the low-caloric bouillon, fruits nd juices.

Nibbling often comes from tension. It can even be an unecognized hunger for exercise, a need for a break in the routine. By jogging in mid-morning, the housewife may find that this abit replaces the snack habit.

DIET TIPS FROM RUNNERS

Runners have some diet habits that joggers can adopt. After heavy workout, particularly on a warm day, runners will drink cup of bouillon. It replaces the salt and satisfies the hunger rge, yet the calorie count is low.

During cross country workouts, or during regular workouts

between meal hours, runners appease the appetite with what th British call "boiled sweets," hard rock grocery store candy wit fruit flavor. A piece or two of the candy won't add many calories while satisfying the need for blood sugar and providing a quic source of energy. Besides, it's inexpensive.

5

IT'S THE PRINCIPLE OF THE THING

As you jog your way to fitness, you are working within a set o proven training methods developed over the past 20 years i the conditioning of some of the world's greatest runners.

Believe it or not, under that flab, you have the same body a the successful runners. Yours just operates physiologically on different plane.

The successful runner has more endurance than you, probabl more speed, better muscle tone and a more efficient cardiovascu lar system as well. And he should, because he's trained regularl and long. His goal is to win races.

Your goal is different. You won't train as hard as the runne and you won't burn up the track with your speed. You will jo for good health, for the extra energy it gives you, for th brighter outlook that comes when you know you look and fee better, and to reduce your waistline and hips, and to slim an firm the legs—for many reasons—all good for you and you family.

TRAINING PRINCIPLES

Here are the training principles. Study them and keep them i mind as you begin your workout schedules.

1. **Train, don't strain:** This is the golden rule of jogging. Neve go all out. Practice Satchel Paige's advice to "just jangle abou loosely." Runners train the year around, yet only about two pe cent of the time do they run at maximum effort. Joggers *neve* run at maximum effort.

2. **Hard-Easy:** This principle works as a rule of life: if yo work hard for a long period, you must rest. The harder you wor the greater the need for rest.

Again, the theme is moderation. In 20 years of trainin national and international runners at the University of Orego it has been found that runners progress more rapidly and painlessly by an alternating program of hard work one day and the next day easy. Chronic fatigue states are avoided.

As mentioned, the jogger's schedule is just a scaled down version of the runner's workout. For example, on his hard days, the runner may put in from six to 15 miles on Monday, Wednesday and Friday. Tuesday and Thursday, the easy days, are for recovery. The workout consists of an easy run of a mile or two plus some walking, jogging and stretching exercises. The runner might add a moderate workout on Saturday or Sunday.

As for joggers: your fitness determines your schedule. If you are a beginning jogger who has been rusting away for years, your hard days may total no more than a half mile. On the recovery days, you may take only a five- or ten-minute walk.

3. **Gradual Stress:** Moderation underlies the principle of gradually increasing stress. The runner who can run a mile in only five minutes does not prepare for a four-minute mile by trying to run one every day. It is conceivable but unlikely that brute force and determination might bring him close to his goal. However, for both runners and joggers, a better, surer way is to advance toward the goal a little bit each day, each week, each month by making use of sound physiological knowledge.

Jogging is a gradual, moderate exercise that permits you to tone up your body while working within your own capability. You tone up your muscles a bit more each day, each week, each month.

The gradual stress principle prevents over-exertion and the danger of an unaccustomed burden on the heart, lungs and other parts of the body.

4. **Appetite or Variety:** Exercise should be interesting. The same exercises done in the same place at the same time every day can bring on indifference. So, it is important to include as much variety as possible. That's what is done in blocking out training programs for runners. In a normal week's schedule, runners can work out on a track or in the hills; they can run fast or slow, repeat certain exercises and do a number of things to test and assess progress.

The jogging schedules offer you an equal variety.

5. **Plan:** Work by plan because some form or order is helpful in most matters. Runners know what they are going to do each day for the month—for three months. Yet the plan is not rigid. It can be modified at any time. Working by plan helps to insure regularity, moderation and variety.

6. **Regularity:** The benefits of exercise are directly related to regularity. Obviously, one week on and one week off won't produce the results that regular exercise will. There are no lasting benefits to health when you exercise for a short time and then stop.

ENLARGED ATHLETIC HEART IS A MYTH

Perhaps at this point you need some assurance about how exercise might affect your heart.

If you're thinking of that old tale about exercise producing enlarged athletic heart, forget it. The enlarged athletic heart is a myth, long ago scientifically disproved.

Instead, envy the athlete with his finely conditioned heart. He built it through regular exercise, the same as you or he would build strong biceps. His heart is super efficient and works far less hard than the average "over 30" heart to accomplish its job.

Even if you've been inactive for 25 years, gradual regular exercise will not damage a normal heart. It will improve it.

6

HOW TO JOG

Joggers come in all shapes and sizes, in a wide range of age levels and varying degrees of fitness. When they set out to jog, their techniques vary greatly.

But, remember, *how you jog is never as important as that you jog*. Performance is what counts. It is always more important than technique.

First, if you are anxious to get going and are bored or discouraged by "how to" instructions, you may want to skim or skip this section for the time being. Later, after you have mastered the routine of jogging, you will enjoy returning to these instructions. Working toward improvement of your form will add new interest to your jogging. *In the meantime, jog away.*

But if you prefer to go at things logically and won't budge from your home without assurance that you are jogging properly, here are some style tips.

1. **Posture:** Stand up straight. Jog that way. Experience with runners proves that for either walking or running, remaining upright is the best posture. It affords the greatest freedom and ease of movement.

Upright means that you should keep your back as straight as naturally comfortable. Keep your head up, neither forward nor back of the body line. Your buttocks should be "tucked in." In this position, a hypothetical line drawn from the top of your head through the shoulders and hips should be perpendicular, or nearly so.

If you have a full length mirror, use it to check your posture. You'll see that if your head and chest are thrust forward, your hips stick out behind.

When jogging do not imitate the military brace where it is good form to throw back the shoulders and stick out the chest. If you do, you're likely to get a muscle ache between the shoulder blades and some discomfort in the lower back. And you will use a lot of energy by unnecessarily contracting a whole series of back muscles. The posture is known as swayback. It is not comfortable, attractive or conducive to good jogging. Remember, you are not in the military. You may do as you like. That thought ought to cheer you.

Another tip: keep your head up and resist the tendency to

watch your feet as you jog. Ask your partner to remind you as soon as your head drops. Do the same for him.

Improved posture may be one of your most valuable rewards from learning to jog. It will carry over into other activities, contributing to your general good looks and physical ability.

2. **Arms:** Your arm movements provide a rhythm that pulls you along. In proper position, the elbows are bent slightly away from the body, neither out like wings nor pressed to the chest. You should develop a habit of proper arm position from the start because it is less tiring over long distances. Do not carry your arms at hip or belt level when you jog.

3. **Legs:** Stand up straight. Your legs should move freely from the hips. The action is easy, not forced. The lift is from the knees, while the ankles remain relaxed. Each foot falls just under the knee. Don't reach out with the foot and overstride.

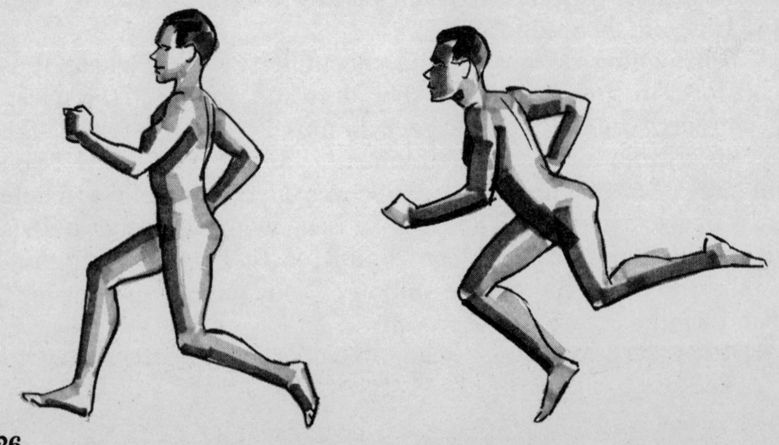

4. **How to Breathe:** Believe it or not, many joggers ask, "Should I breathe with my mouth open?" Emphatically yes! While a moderate activity, jogging does exercise the pulmonary system, working the lungs which inhale and exhale large amounts of air. You won't travel very far breathing daintily through your nose. Open your mouth and take large gulps of air.

HOW TO USE YOUR FEET

Read this material for information. But don't let it make you so self-conscious of arms, legs and feet that you miss the whole point: style should be relaxed and natural.

Footstrike: Part of jogging "know how" is learning the proper way to use your feet.

Footstrike is a term used to describe how your foot hits the ground. Putting foot to track, turf or pavement properly is important because it can provide a lifetime of relaxed running. It also helps avoid some of the soreness that can come from improper technique.

There are three basic methods of footstrike, but no one method that you *must* use. Study each and choose the one that is most comfortable, efficient and works best for you.

Here are the techniques:

1. **Heel-to-toe:** The jogger lands first on the heel of the foot, rocks forward and takes off from the ball of the foot. Hitting with the heel first cushions the landing, then distributes the pressure as the foot bends forward.

Experience shows that this heel-to-toe footstrike is the least tiring over long distances and the least wearing on the rest of

the body. About 70 percent of good long distance runners use this technique.

In a short time, with practice, you may find it the natural way to run.

2. **Flat-foot:** This technique is a variation of the heel-to-toe. Instead of hitting first with the heel, the entire foot lands on the ground at the same time. The wide surface area pillows the footstrike and is easy on the rest of the body.

In the flat-foot technique, the foot falls under the knee in a quick, light action. Don't drive the foot down. Just let it pass beneath the body, then quickly pick it up for the next step. About 20 percent of long distance runners use this technique.

3. **Ball-of-the-foot:** The jogger lands first on the ball of the foot and settles to the heel before taking the next step. Don't be surprised if almost instinctively you start with this method of footstrike, especially if you haven't run since your younger days. The running games you learned as a youngster were almost exclusively sprint games, requiring you to be up on your toes for quick starts. More women than men start with the ball-of-the-foot technique. This is probably because they are used to high heels and find low heels unnatural.

The ball-of-the-foot technique sometimes produces soreness since the muscles must remain in contraction for a longer period of time than heel-to-toe or flat-foot. For some joggers, this method creates a strain that is not as beneficial as the alternating tension and relaxation of the other methods. A little more bend in the knee with each step may help you to get the full foot down on the ground.

RUNNING SURFACES

If there is a large grassy area nearby with no accompanying "keep off" sign, use it for your jogging. It's the best kind of surface because it has some spring in it, some give, that makes it easier on the joints of the ankle and the knee. Where no turfed area is handy, any surface will do, provided you wear the proper shoes. In this case, a proper shoe is one with a sturdy sole and a good cushion inside that will provide an artificial softness.

SHIN SPLINTS OR BUCK SHINS

Beginning joggers and track men who are just beginning training after a long layoff frequently complain of an indisposition known as shin splints or buck shins. This is a soreness in the shin bone, sometimes in the front of the bone, sometimes along the side of the shin. The tenderness comes from a slight tearing of the connective tissue next to the shin bone. While not serious, buck shins are painful. The athlete endures it. The jogger treats it by running for a few days only on soft surfaces until the soreness lets up. Sometimes it is necessary to curtail your jogging for a few days before you can move about in some comfort.

The best preventative is a proper pair of shoes.

7

JOG ANYWHERE—OPEN YOUR DOOR AND YOU'RE IN BUSINESS

Pardon the pun, but you have a running start over your friends and neighbors in other exercise programs. They often need special facilities or equipment or both. You don't.

Jogging country is everywhere. Open your door and you're in business. Jog right out the door, jog in a schoolyard, on a city street, at the beach, on a country road or in a vacant lot. Jog down a bicycle path, on a school track, around a golf course, through a park, in your backyard, in a gymnasium, in a supermarket parking lot—anywhere.

If the weather keeps you indoors, jog in place or move about the house. Take jogging with you on business trips. If you can't get outside, jog in place in your room.

A long carpeted hotel hall is a wonderfully agreeable place for a jog. Track men on a trip out of town often use hotel and motel hallways for light limbering up right before a race or before retiring at night.

To add variety, some joggers have substituted rope skipping for jogging in place. Rope skipping is slightly more strenuous. You judge the amount by the degree of breathlessness that develops.

A MEASURED DISTANCE

Your jogging schedules are based on measured distances developed by training runners on a 440 yard track.

One of the handy and versatile things about jogging is that you don't need a track to measure how far you've traveled. Thousands of people around the country jog in places other than on a track. They gauge their distances, sometimes quite accurately, sometimes roughly, by the following guideposts:

School Track: Most junior high, high school or college tracks are 440 yards in length. Each straightaway and each turn is 110 yards.

Car's Odometer: Many joggers map out courses in their own neighborhood or other places in town by measuring the distance with the car's odometer, using the tenth of a mile in the right hand column. The course possibilities are limitless.

Pedometer: A pedometer is a simple device that will measure how far you've jogged or walked by counting steps. It costs about $8 and is available at most sporting goods stores. The jogger attaches it to his belt or carries it in his hand as he moves along. If you have a boy scout in the family, borrow his. The chances are he's not using it anyway because he doesn't exercise. Bet you've been driving him to the scout meetings.

Stride: You can walk off a course yourself. The average stride is about three feet (one yard).

Telephone pole: In some city neighborhoods and on country roads, telephone poles are good guideposts. An Oregon architect and his wife jog using the poles as distance markers. The poles are approximately 100 yards apart. The architect and his wife jog the distance between two poles, then walk the next.

City Block: There is no standard size city block. To the distress of city governments today, the tough, independent sorts who laid out city streets in the past did so almost by whim. Nevertheless, there is some uniformity. A rough estimate is that the short direction of a city block is 220 feet, and the long side about 400 feet.

Other Guideposts: In the city, in suburbia or in the country, there are lots of guideposts to use to help gauge distances. A West Coast jogger, who as a boy played stickball in the streets of Brooklyn, remembers that manhole covers were used as homeplate and second base. The manhole covers were placed at standard distances, about 100 feet apart. Fire hydrants are another possibility.

On the Trail: On the trail, where there are no guideposts, you can walk along at a pace of about 2½ to 3 miles an hour. If you put your back into it, you can cover about 4 miles in an hour. Using a watch, and estimating that even at a slow jog you will cover twice the ground you will walking, you can get a rough gauge of your distance.

Watches: Unlike time in competitive running, jogging time need not be exact. The jogger is more like the runner during his training period. Then the runner aims for a time range, not an exact time. Wrist watches and pocket watches do nicely for joggers. The dude buys a stop watch.

Hills: Running cross-country and over hills is a wonderful change of pace. But don't try it until your schedule tells you to. And don't blithely attack a hill. As Arthur Lydiard, the New Zealand Olympic coach, is fond of saying, "The hills will find you out." They surely will.

Running up a hill requires a tremendous amount of energy. It also brings into play some muscles you haven't been using while running on the flat. In the training of track men, running the hills is used to build strength and endurance. It also gets them away from the sometimes tedious activity of circling a track.

Running in the hills will do much the same for you. It will build strength and get you away from your regular routine.

One caution: you can legitimately expect some stiff and sore muscles for a day or two after hill running for the first time. The best medicine is to go right on with your regular jogging schedule. It's nothing serious. Be glad you've found those muscles and they still work.

NO EXPENSIVE CLOTHES

Whatever outfit feels comfortable is the one you should wear for jogging. You don't need to be a fashion plate with expensive clothes and footwear. Nearly any comfortable, informal outfit that you already own is appropriate. Your closet and dresser drawers are full of clothes that will do the jog nicely.

CLOTHES DON'T MAKE THE JOGGER BUT THEY MAY HELP THE SPIRIT

The most common jogging outfits are sweatshirts, sweatpants, old sweaters and old trousers. In some communities, joggers have joined together in informal clubs with their own sweatshirts and even jogging caps.

Women seem to perform best when they feel well dressed. So, a bit of style consciousness, providing it doesn't become competitive, is all right. Women who look and feel better in skirts should choose them with enough fullness for freedom of action. In cold weather leotards can be added to the costume. For pants, the stretch knits in cotton, nylon and wool or combinations offer style as well as maximum comfort. Tight contour slacks and snug blue jeans constrict the easy movement desired for jogging.

The ideal costume for either men or women is the warm-up suit such as those worn by athletes; easy fitting stretch pants with matching zippered turtle neck jacket.

DRESS FOR THE SEASON AND THE LOCALE

Obviously, you need to dress for the season and the locale. In general your clothes should be cool during the warmer months and warm when the weather turns cold. In warm weather, a pair of walking or bermuda shorts is ideal, but the shorts should be loose enough to allow easy movement.

Ideally, you should start out with more than one top so that you can shed the outer layer as the exercise progresses. Wear a T-shirt under a sweatshirt or light sweater in warmer weather; a light sweater under a heavier one or jacket in colder weather.

In very cold weather, don't forget gloves and a cap or hood. Cold ears and hands can take some of the fun from the workout.

LONG JOHNS IN COLD WEATHER

You can take advantage of the experience of many joggers who in cold weather like to combine warmth, light weight and easy movement by wearing a pair of cotton long johns under a pair of shorts or trousers or slacks. The cotton is absorbent and comfortable next to the skin. The long johns won't pull away with each step letting in the cold air as trousers or slacks will do.

AVOID RUBBERIZED OR PLASTIC CLOTHES

Avoid the unnecessary discomfort that comes from wearing rubberized or plastic clothes that cause sweating and high body heat. You gain nothing and the dehydration brings on muscle cramps and fatigue. Essentially, plastic and rubber clothes prevent evaporation of perspiration which is nature's way of adjusting body temperature.

Some joggers may mistakenly use them with the idea of losing weight. They cause only a temporary loss of salt and water due to perspiration. Permanent loss results only from burning up calories.

THE SHOES SHOULD FIT

If your feet are going to carry you to fitness, they must be treated well. Your shoes are an important item. A number of firms specializing in sporting goods make shoes especially for track and long distance running. You may purchase a pair or get by nicely with what you have at home.

As you grow older, your foot needs an extra cushion.

In general, shoes should be sturdy with rubber, crepe, ripple or neolite sole. Probably the shoes you wear for gardening, working in the shop or around the house will do just fine.

Sneakers and tennis shoes are all right if they are the heavy variety. The fashionable, light weight "tennies" that school girls and some housewives wear won't hold up or provide the comfort you require for jogging.

8

JOGGING PLANS MATCH YOUR FITNESS

There are three jogging plans that roughly match three broad categories of adult physical fitness. Each plan has a special schedule that permits a jogger to begin at his own level of physical fitness.

Check the description at the beginning of each plan to see which you should follow.

Plan A: About 10 percent of the men and about 30 percent of the women who begin jogging are below average physical fitness and need to increase their activity more gradually. Plan A permits them to begin at a modest level, and when successful, move up to Plan B.

Plan B: Plan B is suitable for the majority of men and women of any age. About 80 percent of the men and 60 percent of the women who begin jogging can use this plan comfortably.

Plan C: Another 10 percent of both men and women have a higher level of physical fitness. Plan C takes this into consideration and provides a somewhat stronger program.

ASSESSING PROGRESS

To get the most from the jogging program, you should periodically assess your progress. Unlike the runner, you may have to be your own coach and trainer.

Begin the assessment by being honest with yourself. Take your psychological pulse as well as your heartbeat.

Are you normally timid and do less than required? If so, you may have to push yourself a bit.

Or are you a tiger, biting off more than you can chew? If yes, then hold yourself in check.

Remember, it will take two or three months of training to improve your physical condition. Take it easy at the start and don't overdo. Consider that you are *in training to develop a habit of permanent moderate exercise.*

Permanent is the key word. If you have a temporary setback, don't quit. Your schedule is flexible and makes allowances. Keep jogging.

PROGRESS CHART

To get the fullest enjoyment from jogging, keep a record. Mark down everything as follows:

1. Each day enter the jogging schedule completed as 1-M, 1-F, or 3-W, meaning you have completed Monday of the first week, Friday of the first week and Wednesday of the third week.
2. Mark an "0" in the square if you completely miss a day.
3. Mark "X" on easy days of stretching and short walks.
4. Mark 1½, 2, or any number that approximates the distance in miles done on optional days of Saturday or Sunday.

Reminder: Before you begin the jogging program, and regularly on the first day of each month thereafter, enter your measurements in pounds and inches in the proper spaces.

MONTHS

	J	F	M	A	M	J	J	A	S	O	N	D
1												
2												
3												
4												
5												
6												
7												
8												
9												
10												
11												
12												
13												
14												
15												
16												
17												
18												
19												
20												
21												
22												
23												
24												
25												
26												
27												
28												
29												
30												
31												

Total miles per month

	J	F	M	A	M	J	J	A	S	O	N	D
1												
1												
1												
1												
1												

Ht. ______________

Before	After	
		Weight
		Girth of abdomen
		Girth of chest (resting expiration)
		Girth right mid-thigh
		Girth hips

JOGGING WITH COMPANIONS

If possible, jog with someone of the same ability. But most important, be content to jog at your own pace. If your buddy wants to run faster, suggest instead that he run further. If he just runs faster, he completes his distance, then stops and waits. As you puff up to him, he's had a rest and is ready to go again. Let him run further and then back to you. Enjoy the walking period together.

Jogging is *never* competitive. If you want to compete, do it against your own inertia on the days when you don't want to go out or tackle a new assignment.

HOW TO CHANGE PLANS

Anytime you want to, you can change plans. Go up or down, depending on your need and a frank evaluation of your condition. A simple rule is to move to a workout in the new plan that requires the same distance as your present plan. For example, if you are jogging one mile in Plan A and feel the need for a more vigorous schedule, move to a week in Plan B that also calls for one mile. Similarly, if you wish to drop back from Plan B to Plan A, move to a week in Plan A that requires the same distance.

THE GAMES JOGGERS PLAY— I'M 10 MILES EAST OF DUBUQUE

Remember the armchair strategists of World War II? Pins and small flags in maps? When the Allies moved, the pins and flags went with them. The hated enemy was watched as well. Then V-E and V-J days.

What's become of the strategists? Many, older and wiser, are joggers. Still they plot with pin and flag. The keen eye—the experience are not lost or wasted. Now they plot their own moves.

The miles add up when jogging regularly. The former strategist picks a goal and starts out jogging. The pins move. Cross-country trips are not uncommon. The Southwest is popular during the Winter months.

One jogger headed north on Interstate 5 from Eugene, Oregon, turned east at Portland, made two trips around Mt. Hood, then hurled himself eastward. At publication time, more fit than ever, he reported, "I'm ten miles east of Dubuque."

Where will jogging take you? Quick—get the map and pins. Don't miss a mile.

Have you been to Alaska?

9

JOGGER'S RECONDITIONING PROGRAM

Reconditioning here refers to a set of guidelines for joggers and runners who miss their regular schedules because of illness or sore muscles.

As mentioned, joggers follow a scaled-down version of the training program used by University of Oregon runners. Consequently, both joggers and runners have experienced the same kinds of minor disabilities: sore feet, sore Achilles tendons, shin splints, aching back and sore calf and thigh muscles.

The simple and effective rehabilitation instructions listed here are based on 20 years of experience in literally putting runners and joggers back on their feet. No matter what your level of fitness, the instructions apply.

1. Observe the Golden Rule of Jogging: **TRAIN, DON'T STRAIN.**
2. When soreness is not severe, keep jogging. Don't quit. The soreness will just recur if you don't continue. Rather, drop back two or three weeks in your schedule. Do less work, but continue to work out by a schedule. Or, if you are brand new to jogging, follow Rule 4.
3. Jog on soft surfaces. The natural cushion of grass, or leaves and pine needles absorbs the shock and lessens the discomfort. When you can not find a soft surface, create one by wearing properly cushioned shoes.
4. When soreness is severe, or if you are brand new to jogging, limit your exercise to walking, but do your walking by a schedule.
5. Workouts should be enjoyable. If soreness is too severe, you may have to retire for a week or two. You are the best judge of your threshold of pain.
6. **MAKE HASTE SLOWLY.** Stay on the reconditioning plan as long as needed.
7. When you are ready to return to regular jogging, pick a

schedule at *today's* lesser level of fitness and work up. Don't hurry. You have a lifetime in which to improve fitness.

8. When you develop a cold, an upper respiratory ailment or any illness, **DO NOT JOG.** When the condition clears, begin jogging at *today's* lesser level of fitness.

9. When in doubt, check first with your physician. If you have any unusual or persistent pain, go see him.

STRETCHING EXERCISES TO ACCOMPANY PLANS A, B AND C

Jogging is directed at exercising the heart and lungs. As you jog you exercise other muscles as well. The legs, arms and gluteal muscles (buttocks) are exercised vigorously.

A good companion to jogging is a set of easy stretching movements designed to loosen bunched-up, tense muscles in the neck, chest, abdomen and back. These are not quick, pulling motions, but gradual, easy freeing-up exercises.

On the days when jogging is not scheduled, do the exercises as you stroll. On jogging days, do them as you catch your breath while walking.

1. Loosen your neck and roll your head in a wide circle. Repeat two or three times to limber up tensed muscles in the cervical area (upper spine). A great deal of bad posture comes from tension.

2. Raise your shoulders and roll them forward, then around to loosen the back muscles and the pectoral muscles of the chest. Repeat two or three times.

3. Easily move your shoulders forward and toward the middle as though trying to make them meet; then reverse and stretch them backward trying to make the wings touch. Repeat two or three times.

4. While walking, stick out the abdomen, then suck it in and roll the hips forward. Repeat two or three times.

Do these exercises continuously while walking on both jogging and non-jogging days.

LOW BACK PAIN

Among the "over 30" low back pain is a common complaint. When the cause is bad posture from poor muscle tone the following exercises will help:

1. **Straight back.** Stand with your back to the wall or some other flat surface. Place your heels about four inches from the wall and bend the knees slightly. Now tighten the abdominals and roll the hips forward (tilt the pelvis). Your back is now straight up and down against the wall. With muscles tight and back straight, walk four or five steps from the wall. Relax. Let the sag come back. Repeat not more than five times.

By improving the tone of the abdominal muscles, you will keep the hips in position and automatically improve posture.

2. **Straight back variation.** Lie on the floor on your back, legs out straight. Now tighten the abdominal muscles and tilt the pelvis forward. (Flatten the small of the back.) Keep the abdominal muscles tight and slowly count to five. Then slowly bring in the right leg, keeping the foot on the floor. Do the same with the left leg. Relax. Repeat not more than five times.

3. **Middle-age hunch—round shoulders.** This exercise will put some elasticity back into the neck and shoulder muscles. It can result in improved posture. Lie on the floor with shoulders and neck as flat as possible, arms out flat on the floor. Slowly bring up the arms and tense the muscles as though pulling a heavy weight. Drop the arms slowly as though pulling down a heavy weight.

JOGGING AT HIGH ALTITUDES

Whatever you do, don't start a new jogging program while on a trip to Cheyenne, Wyoming or Gartok, Tibet, without being aware of the altitude and its effects on the body.

People react differently to changes in altitude. Generally speaking, a move to a high elevation from a location close to sea level puts an extra burden on the respiratory and circulatory system. With time, the systems adjust to working in an atmosphere with less oxygen than they are used to. How long the adjustment takes varies from person to person.

The subject of the effects of vigorous exercise on the performance of athletes, and even on their health, is much in the news because the 1968 Olympics are scheduled for the rarefied atmosphere of Mexico City. Physiologists, coaches, physicians frankly admit that they do not completely understand the complicated physiological changes that take place at higher altitudes.

Some controlled research with athletes shows that the physical mechanism needs at least six weeks to adjust to a change to high altitude. After that time, the athlete can perform up to his customary level of effort without undue strain or uncomfortable effects. For example, a runner who consistently runs a mile in 4:00 to 4:03 minutes in Eugene, Oregon, elevation 375 feet, can put out the same effort in Mexico City if he has conditioned himself properly at 6,000 feet.

So to the jogger, a word of caution. If you are leaving on a trip to Chile or Tibet, don't *begin* a jogging career now. Wait until you return to your normal level.

If you are a well-seasoned jogger, by all means continue your routine. Just scale it down when you are in high country. If shortness of breath slows you to a walk, don't be alarmed—just walk until you are breathing easily, as you did when you first started jogging.

Finally, people have different levels of tolerance for altitude. Some feel better in the mountains, some at sea level. A few people never adjust to altitudes above 5,000 feet. So, for joggers who move from one altitude to another, the advice is simply to remember the principles of the activity: measure your ability, limitations, needs and goals and adjust the jogging program to fit them.

PACE CHART

Runners train both on and off the track. Off-the-track training usually includes cross-country running to build strength and endurance. In this kind of training, the runner seldom concerns himself with the pace, the speed at which he is running. When he trains on the track, his attitude changes. Pace is quite important. Because he competes on the track, the runner must be able to judge how fast he is going. If he goes too fast or faster than his capability, he will experience "oxygen debt" and pay the price in the late stages of the race by running out of steam.

Joggers also need to develop a sense of pace. The jogger who runs too fast will abuse himself as well as pay the "oxygen debt." The Pace Chart should help you understand what it's all about. For example, at 15 minutes per mile, about the pace of a good walk, the jogger will cover 55 yards in 28 seconds. He allows himself a margin of error of about five seconds fast or slow permitting him to run the 55 yards in from 25-30 seconds. As he becomes a good judge of pace, the jogger will come much closer to the 28 seconds.

Pace Chart

	Pace for Mile	*55 Yds.*	*110 Yds.*	*220 Yds.*	*440 yds. ¼ mi.*	*880 yds. ½ mi.*	*¾ mi.*
Pace 1	15 min.	28 sec.	56 sec.	1 min. 52	3 min. 45	7 min. 30	11 min. 15
		25-30	55-60	1:45-2:00	3:40-3:50	7:25-7:35	11:10-11:20
	14 min.	26	52	1:45	3:30	7:00	10:30
	13 min.	24	48	1:37	3:15	6:30	9:45
Pace 2	12 min.	22	45	1:30	3:00	6:00	9:00
	11 min.	21	42	1:22	2:45	5:30	8:15
Pace 3	10 min.	18	37	1:15	2:30	5:00	7:30
	9 min.	17	34	68	2:15	4:30	6:45
Pace 4	8 min.	15	30	60	2:00	4:00	6:00
	Now you are ½ as fast as a 4 minute miler						
Pace 5	7 min.	13	26	53	1:45	3:30	5:15

Faster than 7 minutes per mile is a run, not a jog

10
PLAN A

Experience shows that even after years of inactivity, adults can recapture a high degree of physical fitness. But they need time in which to do it. They also need a special program that begins at their *present* level of physical fitness or unfitness. The program must have built-in patience.

In selecting your conditioning plan, evaluate your physical condition frankly. Try not to let your emotions influence you. If you overdo at first, you may receive a setback or even harm yourself. Athletes who are in good condition at the start, take months to train themselves to a higher level of fitness.

Plan A results from years of research with joggers. It has the special ingredients that will help those who now cannot profit from Plan B.

WHO USES PLAN A

Broadly speaking, Plan A joggers are among the following:

(1) *The inactive person* who has led a totally sedentary life. He seldom walks when he can ride. He has an automatic tuning device on his TV set. He never golfs, bowls, rows a boat or plays tennis. He works all day at his desk and has an inefficient cardiovascular system from long-term inactivity.

He can improve his fitness but he must start slowly.

(2) *The person who has just recovered from an illness or an accident* or who has spent a prolonged time in bed. Frequently mild exercise is prescribed for his rehabilitation. This mild jogging program is just the ticket. However, anyone attempting any exercise after an illness or accident should first get his physician's approval.

(3) *The obese person* who is 20 percent over his desired weight (see page 19 for Metropolitan weight charts). He chooses Plan A because his cardiovascular system is suspect. Also, because his feet, joints and leg muscles need conditioning before he can tackle a more active program.

LOOKING AHEAD

After completing Plan A, some joggers move to Plan B and work toward an even higher level of fitness. Other Plan A joggers improve so rapidly that they move to Plan B before completing the entire 12 weeks (see page 36 for instructions for changing plans). Still others in Plan A complete the program and are satisfied to remain at their new found level of physical fitness.

Jogging plans are flexible. If you are slow to get in shape, stay on the same schedule as long as you need to. If you blossom quickly and work up an appetite for a stronger plan, try one. Jogging always lets you work within your own capability.

Plan A

FOR MEN AND WOMEN IN LESS THAN AVERAGE PHYSICAL CONDITION

Week I

If you've been inactive for a long time, it may take awhile to scrape away the rust. Don't hurry. Make haste slowly.

Experience shows that for the first couple of weeks, Plan A joggers perform best on a schedule that requires about one-half the stress of Plan B.

You have three scheduled workouts this week and every week (hard-easy principle). If you were in Plan B you covered a mile in each workout, so your distance in Plan A is one-half mile.

If the first day's schedule seems too long, do only as much of it as is comfortable. Gradually increase the distance until you can do the regular schedule without strain, then follow the regular Plan A.

If the first two or three workouts seem too difficult, you may need an even more gradual conditioning program. *See the Walker-Jogger Program*, page 68, at the end of Plan A.

Here are some points to keep in mind as you begin the first Plan A workout:

1. Although the schedules are arranged for Monday, Wednesday and Friday, the days are not compulsory. Use Tuesday, Thursday and Saturday if you wish. Just remember the "hard-easy" principle: exercise one day, rest the next.

2. Start at a moderate speed. Almost without exception, joggers begin by running too fast. They develop sore muscles the next day. Jogging for beginners is slow, just faster than a walk.

3. To find the right beginning pace, try the "talk test." If jogging 55 yards leaves you gasping and too breathless to talk with your companions, you're going too fast. Slow down or walk.

4. Finish your workout exhilarated and not exhausted. Don't do too much the first day and end up with sore muscles. Remember, there are years of pleasant workouts ahead of you.

5. Mark down your performance on the Progress Chart.

Week I

Pace 1 = 110 yds. at 55 to 60 seconds, or 25 to 30 seconds for 55 yds.

			Pace
Monday			
(total distance: ½ mile)			
(1) Jog 55 yds.	Walk 55 yds.	4 times	1
(2) Jog 110 yds.	Walk 110 yds.		1
(3) Jog 55 yds	Walk 55 yds.	2 times	1

Tuesday 5 to 10 minute walk; easy stretching exercises

Wednesday			
(total distance: ½ mile)			
(1) Jog 55 yds.	Walk 55 yds.	4 times	1
(2) Jog 110 yds.	Walk 110 yds.		1
(3) Jog 55 yds.	Walk 55 yds.	2 times	1

Thursday 5 to 10 minute walk; easy stretching exercises

Friday			
(total distance: ½ mile)			
(1) Jog 55 yds.	Walk 55 yds.	4 times	1
(2) Jog 110 yds.	Walk 110 yds.		1
(3) Jog 55 yds.	Walk 55 yds.	2 times	1

Saturday 5 to 10 minute walk; change the scenery

Sunday 5 to 10 minute walk; easy stretching exercises

Week II

As mentioned, your schedule is a scaled-down version of a training pattern that has produced thousands of contented joggers as well as a long list of international track and field champions at the University of Oregon.

As part of the pattern for both joggers and runners, the schedules are arranged so that the distance and pace are increased by plan.

This week, you will add ½ mile for a total of ¾ of a mile in each workout. Everything else is the same as the first week. After 12 weeks on Plan A, you walk and jog 1½ miles comfortably at a brisk pace. But begin slowly.

1. If you find the schedule too strenuous and develop aches and pains and sore joints, don't lay off. The problem will just recur. Rather, cut down the distance or the speed. Running on a soft surface will help relieve the aches and pains (see Reconditioning, page 37).

2. Another possible pain is muscle cramps or spasms. You may need more salt. Take some unless you specifically have been advised not to take salt.

3. If after cutting down the distance and speed, you still find the schedule too strenuous, *walk through the exercises*. At the end of the second week's schedule, take your psychological pulse. Be honest with yourself. Is your inability to complete the schedule real or imaginary? Take another look at the *Walker-Jogger Program*. Remember, train, don't strain.

Week II

Pace 1 = 110 yds. at 55 to 60 seconds, or 25 to 30 seconds for 55 yds.

			Pace
Monday			
(total distance: ¾ mile)			
(1) Jog 55 yds.	Walk 55 yds.	4 times	1
(2) Jog 110 yds.	Walk 110 yds.	2 times	1
(3) Jog 55 yds.	Walk 55 yds.	4 times	1

Tuesday 5 to 10 minute walk; easy stretching exercises

Wednesday			
(total distance: ¾ mile)			
(1) Jog 55 yds.	Walk 55 yds.	3 times	1
(2) Jog 110 yds.	Walk 110 yds.	3 times	1
(3) Jog 55 yds.	Walk 55 yds.	3 times	1

Thursday 5 to 10 minute walk; easy stretching exercises

Friday			
(total distance: ¾ mile)			
(1) Jog 55 yds.	Walk 55 yds.	4 times	1
(2) Jog 110 yds.	Walk 110 yds.	2 times	1
(3) Jog 55 yds.	Walk 55 yds.	4 times	1

Saturday 5 to 10 minute walk; change the scenery

Sunday 5 to 10 minute walk; easy stretching exercises

Week III

This week increase the distance to 1 mile. Increase the pace slightly as well.

1. On the second day of the schedule, you have your first try at New Zealand fartlek. This is slow, *steady* jogging for as long as you comfortably can. With steady jogging, the pace is quite slow, probably slower than you think you should run. Certainly slower than the pace you use during interval jogging. Use the "talk test" to check your pace.

Oregon runners and joggers use another device as part of their training plan. They carry out specified kinds of exercise on given days. For example, you and the runners have three workouts each week.

On Monday, you will do *only* interval work (alternate jogging and walking at different distances).

On Wednesday, you will do New Zealand fartlek (slow steady jogging).

On Friday, you will do a combination of interval and fartlek jogging.

You will follow this part of the plan for the next 10 weeks.

Don't forget the walking and stretching on Tuesday and Thursday.

Week III

Pace 1 = 110 yds. at 55 to 60 seconds
Pace 2 = 110 yds. at 45 to 50 seconds

			Pace
Monday			
(total distance: 1 mile)			
(1) Jog 55 yds.	Walk 55 yds.	4 times	2
(2) Jog 220 yds.	Walk 220 yds.		2
(3) Jog 110 yds.	Walk 110 yds.	2 times	2
(4) Jog 55 yds.	Walk 55 yds.	4 times	2

Tuesday 5 to 10 minute walk; easy stretching exercises

Wednesday			
(total distance: 1 mile)			
(1) Jog 55 yds.	Walk 55 yds.	4 times	2
(2) Steady, slow fartlek jog for 2 or 3 minutes. The pace is 55 to 75 seconds for 110 yds. Walk when you need to. Jog again for a sustained 2 or 3 minutes.			
(3) Jog 55 yds.	Walk 55 yds.	4 times	2

Thursday 5 to 10 minute walk; easy stretching exercises

Friday			
(total distance: 1 mile)			
(1) Jog 55 yds.	Walk 55 yds.	2 times	2
(2) Jog 110 yds.	Walk 110 yds.		2
(3) Fartlek jog for a sustained 2 or 3 minutes. Walk until recovered.			
(4) Jog 55 yds.	Walk 55 yds.	4 times	2

Saturday 5 to 10 minute walk; change the scenery

Sunday 5 to 10 minute walk; easy stretching exercises

Week IV

The distance is 1 mile.

The schedule is quite similar to last week's: interval work the first day, New Zealand fartlek the second day and a combination of interval and fartlek on the third day.

How is your technique? Easy and natural? If not, perhaps you should reread the paragraphs on "How to Jog."

Mark your performance on the Progress Chart.

Week IV

Pace 1 = 110 yds. at 55 to 60 seconds
Pace 2 = 110 yds. at 45 to 50 seconds

				Pace
Monday				
(total distance: 1 mile)				
(1)	Jog 110 yds.	Walk 110 yds.	4 times	2
(2)	Jog 220 yds.	Walk 220 yds.		2
(3)	Jog 110 yds.	Walk 110 yds.	2 times	2

Tuesday 5 to 10 minute walk; easy stretching exercises

Wednesday				
(total distance: 1 mile)				
(1)	Jog 110 yds.	Walk 110 yds.	2 times	2
(2)	Slow steady fartlek, 2 or 3 minutes. Walk until recovered. Repeat once.			
(3)	Jog 55 yds.	Walk 55 yds.	4 times	2

Thursday 5 to 10 minute walk; easy stretching exercises

Friday				
(total distance: 1 mile)				
(1)	Jog 55 yds.	Walk 55 yds.	2 times	2
(2)	Jog 110 yds.	Walk 110 yds.		2
(3)	Slow fartlek jog for 2 or 3 minutes.			
(4)	Jog 55 yds.	Walk 55 yds.	4 times	2

Saturday 5 to 10 minute walk; change the scenery

Sunday 5 to 10 minute walk; easy stretching exercises

Week V

This week the distance is 1 mile for each workout. Some advice: whenever a schedule seems particularly difficult, do *not* advance to the next one. Rather, stay with the present schedule until you can complete it comfortably, or drop back a week. Stay there until you are ready to move up again.

Perhaps you've noticed that the shortest interval is now 110 yds. You've graduated from the 55 yd. intervals. Congratulations.

Hungry after a workout? See "Diet Tips from Runners," p. 21.

Optional Program. Your fitness has improved over the last 5 weeks. You should now consider an optional program designed to increase gradually your total distance each week. On Saturday or Sunday, not both, take a long walk or do some slow jogging for ½ to 1 mile. Change the scenery. Make it a holiday.

Week V

Pace 1 = 110 yds. at 55 to 60 seconds
Pace 2 = 110 yds. at 45 to 50 seconds

Monday
(total distance: 1 mile)

				Pace
(1)	Jog 110 yds.	Walk 110 yds.	2 times	2
(2)	Jog 220 yds.	Walk 220 yds.	2 times	2
(3)	Jog 110 yds.	Walk 110 yds.	2 times	2

Tuesday 5 to 10 minute walk; easy stretching exercises

Wednesday
(total distance: 1 mile)

				Pace
(1)	Jog 110 yds.	Walk 110 yds.	2 times	2
(2)	Slow fartlek jog for 2 or 3 minutes, walk and repeat.			
(3)	Jog 110 yds.	Walk 110 yds.	2 times	2

Thursday 5 to 10 minute walk; easy stretching exercises

Friday
(total distance: 1 mile)

				Pace
(1)	Jog 110 yds.	Walk 110 yds.	2 times	2
(2)	Slow fartlek jog for 2 or 3 minutes.			
(3)	Jog 110 yds.	Walk 110 yds.	2 times	2
(4)	Jog 55 yds.	Walk 55 yds.	4 times	2

Saturday Consider optional program today or tomorrow—not both

Sunday Optional program or 10 minute walk; stretching exercises

Week VI

Add ¼ mile for a total distance of 1¼ miles for each workout. Increase the pace slightly. You have continued variety in your workouts: intervals on Monday; fartlek on Wednesday; intervals and fartlek on Friday. If aches and pains develop, see the Reconditioning Plan, p. 37.

Don't forget the Progress Chart.

Week VI

Pace 2 = 110 yds. at 45 to 50 seconds
Pace 3 = 110 yds. at 35 to 40 seconds

			Pace
Monday			
(total distance: 1¼ miles)			
(1) Jog 110 yds.	Walk 110 yds.	4 times	2 or 3
(2) Jog 220 yds.	Walk 220 yds.	2 times	2 or 3
(3) Jog 110 yds.	Walk 110 yds.	2 times	2 or 3

Tuesday 5 to 10 minute walk; easy stretching exercises

Wednesday
(total distance: 1¼ miles)

(1) Jog 110 yds.	Walk 110 yds.	2 times	2 or 3
(2) Slow fartlek jog for 3 or 4 minutes, walk and repeat.			
(3) Jog 110 yds.	Walk 110 yds.	2 times	2 or 3

Thursday 5 to 10 minute walk; easy stretching exercises

Friday
(total distance: 1¼ miles)

(1) Jog 110 yds.	Walk 110 yds.	2 times	2 or 3
(2) Slow fartlek jog for 3 or 4 minutes.			
(3) Jog 220 yds.	Walk 220 yds.		2 or 3
(4) Jog 110 yds.	Walk 110 yds.	2 times	2 or 3

Saturday Consider optional program today or tomorrow—not both

Sunday Optional program or 10 minute walk; stretching exercises

Week VII

The distance is $1\frac{1}{4}$ miles again. The pace is the same as last week. Remember, on the days that jogging is not scheduled, you should spend 10 to 15 minutes walking and stretching. Don't hurry things. Train, don't strain.

Week VII

Pace 2 = 110 yds. at 45 to 50 seconds
Pace 3 = 110 yds. at 35 to 40 seconds

Monday
(total distance: 1¼ miles)

				Pace
(1)	Jog 110 yds.	Walk 110 yds.	2 times	2 or 3
(2)	Jog 220 yds.	Walk 220 yds.		2 or 3
(3)	Jog 330 yds.	Walk 110 yds.		2 or 3
(4)	Jog 110 yds.	Walk 110 yds.	4 times	2 or 3

Tuesday 5 to 10 minute walk; easy stretching exercises

Wednesday
(total distance: 1¼ miles)

				Pace
(1)	Jog 110 yds.	Walk 110 yds.	2 times	2 or 3
(2)	Slow fartlek jog for 3 or 4 minutes, walk and repeat.			
(3)	Jog 110 yds.	Walk 110 yds.	2 times	2 or 3

Thursday 5 to 10 minute walk; easy stretching exercises

Friday
(total distance: 1¼ miles)

				Pace
(1)	Jog 110 yds.	Walk 110 yds.	2 times	2 or 3
(2)	Slow fartlek jog for 3 or 4 minutes.			
(3)	Jog 220 yds.	Walk 220 yds.		2 or 3
(4)	Jog 110 yds.	Walk 110 yds.	2 times	2 or 3

Saturday Consider optional program today or tomorrow—not both

Sunday Optional program or 10 minute walk; stretching exercises

Week VIII

The distance is $1\frac{1}{4}$ miles.

Possibly you've found Plan A too easy and want more challenge. Since you're running $1\frac{1}{4}$ miles on the Plan A schedule, move to the same distance in Plan B. It is always better to begin cautiously and move up than to be overambitious at the start and later suffer the disappointment of dropping back. If you have a reasonable doubt about your ability to handle the schedule in Plan B, stay with Plan A for two more weeks. You be the judge.

Use the *Optional Plan* on Saturday or Sunday, not both days

Week VIII

Pace 2 = 110 yds. at 45 to 50 seconds
Pace 3 = 110 yds. at 35 to 40 seconds

			Pace
Monday			
(total distance: 1¼ miles)			
(1) Jog 110 yds.	Walk 110 yds.	3 times	2 or 3
(2) Jog 220 yds.	Walk 110 yds.	2 times	2 or 3
(3) Jog 330 yds.	Walk 110 yds.	2 times	2 or 3
(4) Jog 110 yds.	Walk 110 yds.		2 or 3

Tuesday 5 to 10 minute walk; easy stretching exercises

Wednesday			
(total distance: 1¼ miles)			
(1) Jog 110 yds.	Walk 110 yds.	2 times	2 or 3
(2) Slow fartlek jog for 3 or 4 minutes; walk and repeat.			
(3) Jog 110 yds.	Walk 110 yds.	2 times	2 or 3

Thursday 5 to 10 minute walk; easy stretching exercises

Friday			
(total distance: 1¼ miles)			
(1) Jog 110 yds.	Walk 110 yds.	2 times	2 or 3
(2) Slow fartlek jog for 3 or 4 minutes			
(3) Jog 220 yds.	Walk 110 yds.	2 times	2 or 3
(4) Jog 110 yds	Walk 110 yds.	3 times	2 or 3

Saturday Consider optional program today or tomorrow—not both

Sunday Optional program or 10 minute walk; stretching exercises

Week IX

Add ¼ mile for a total distance of 1½ miles for each workout.

Joggers get their first big charge from improved fitness at about six weeks. At nine weeks the feeling of wellbeing grows. Look at your schedule. You began at a half mile, now you're jogging a mile and a half, and you've picked up the pace considerably. You've advanced your level of physical fitness. Your heart has adapted itself to the amount of exercise required of it. The tone and elasticity of your entire cardiovascular system are up, and your lungs now handle a greater volume of oxygen. Keep it up. Check the Progress Chart.

Week IX

Pace 3 = 110 yds. at 35 to 40 seconds

Monday
(total distance: 1½ miles)

				Pace
(1)	Jog 110 yds.	Walk 110 yds.	3 times	3
(2)	Jog 220 yds.	Walk 110 yds.	2 times	3
(3)	Jog 330 yds.	Walk 110 yds.	2 times	3
(4)	Jog 110 yds.	Walk 110 yds.	2 times	3

Tuesday 5 to 10 minute walk; easy stretching exercises

Wednesday
(total distance: 1½ miles)

(1)	Jog 110 yds.	Walk 110 yds.	2 times	3
(2)	Fartlek jog, walk and recover.		3 times	
(3)	Jog 110 yds.	Walk 110 yds.	2 times	3

Thursday 5 to 10 minute walk; easy stretching exercises

Friday
(total distance: 1½ miles)

(1)	Jog 110 yds.	Walk 110 yds.	2 times	3
(2)	Slow fartlek jog for 4 or 5 minutes.			
(3)	Jog 110 yds.	Walk 110 yds.	4 times	3

Saturday Consider optional program today or tomorrow—not both

Sunday Optional program or 10 minute walk; stretching exercises

Week X

The distance is $1\frac{1}{2}$ miles. Everything is about the same as last week.

As you come to the last weeks, the schedules reach a plateau. The distance remains the same each week. Only the pace changes.

You are now reaching the ceiling of your ability in this schedule. Remaining at the same distance for a couple weeks helps you build a tolerance while you decide whether you wish to remain at this level of fitness, move ahead or drop back.

You'll make the decision in two more weeks.

Remember to check the Progress Chart. Train, don't strain.

Week X

Pace 3 = 110 yds. at 35 to 40 seconds

Monday
(total distance: 1½ miles)

	Jog	Walk	Times	*Pace*
(1)	Jog 110 yds.	Walk 110 yds.	2 times	3
(2)	Jog 330 yds.	Walk 110 yds.	2 times	3
(3)	Jog 220 yds.	Walk 110 yds.	3 times	3
(4)	Jog 110 yds.	Walk 110 yds.	2 times	3

Tuesday 5 to 10 minute walk; easy stretching exercises

Wednesday
(total distance: 1½ miles)

	Jog	Walk	Times	Pace
(1)	Jog 110 yds.	Walk 110 yds.	2 times	3
(2)	Slow fartlek jog for 4 or 5 minutes, walk and repeat.			
(3)	Jog 110 yds.	Walk 110 yds.	2 times	3

Thursday 5 to 10 minute walk; easy stretching exercises

Friday
(total distance: 1½ miles)

	Jog	Walk	Times	Pace
(1)	Jog 220 yds.	Walk 110 yds.	2 times	3
(2)	Slow fartlek jog for 4 or 5 minutes.			
(3)	Jog 110 yds.	Walk 110 yds.	2 times	3

Saturday Consider optional program today or tomorrow—not both

Sunday Optional program or 10 minute walk; stretching exercises

Week XI

Again, the distance is 1½ miles, but the pace picks up. Give some more thought about what you're going to do at the completion of this plan.

Remember the walking and stretching on Tuesday and Thursday.

Week XI

Pace 3 = 110 yds. at 35 to 40 seconds
Pace 4 = 110 yds. at 25 to 30 seconds

Monday
(total distance: $1\frac{1}{2}$ miles)

				Pace
(1)	Jog 110 yds.	Walk 110 yds.	2 times	3 or 4
(2)	Jog 330 yds.	Walk 110 yds.	2 times	3 or 4
(3)	Jog 220 yds.	Walk 110 yds.	2 times	3 or 4
(4)	Jog 110 yds.	Walk 110 yds.	3 times	3 or 4

Tuesday 5 to 10 minute walk; easy stretching exercises

Wednesday
(total distance: $1\frac{1}{2}$ miles)

(1) Jog 110 yds. Walk 110 yds. 2 times 3 or 4
(2) Slow fartlek jog for 4 to 6 minutes, walk and repeat.
(3) Jog 110 yds. Walk 110 yds. 2 times 3 or 4

Thursday 5 to 10 minute walk; easy stretching exercises

Friday
(total distance: $1\frac{1}{2}$ miles)

(1) Jog 110 yds. Walk 110 yds. 2 times 3 or 4
(2) Jog 220 yds. Walk 110 yds. 2 times 3 or 4
(3) Slow fartlek jog 4 to 6 minutes.
(4) Jog 110 yds. Walk 110 yds. 2 times 3 or 4

Saturday Consider optional program today or tomorrow—not both

Sunday Optional program or 10 minute walk; stretching exercises

Week XII

The distance is $1\frac{1}{2}$ miles at a good pace.

This is the last week of Plan A. Congratulations on coming this far. If you're a typical jogger, you've now trained yourself up to a level of fitness you thought you'd lost forever.

Now you've got three choices. You can move up to the slightly more strenuous exercises of Plan B and work toward a higher level of fitness. You can maintain the present level or drop back.

You are the best judge of what level is best for you.

You have a wonderful start toward developing a *habit of permanent moderate exercise.* No matter what kind of setback you experience, you can always recondition yourself through the flexible jogging program.

Week XII

Pace 3 = 110 yds. at 35 to 40 seconds
Pace 4 = 110 yds. at 25 to 30 seconds

			Pace
Monday (total distance: 1½ miles)			
(1) Jog 110 yds.	Walk 110 yds.		3 or 4
(2) Jog 220 yds.	Walk 110 yds.	2 times	3 or 4
(3) Jog 330 yds.	Walk 110 yds.	3 times	3 or 4
(4) Jog 110 yds.	Walk 110 yds.	2 times	3 or 4

Tuesday 5 to 10 minute walk; easy stretching exercises

Wednesday (total distance: 1½ miles)			
(1) Jog 110 yds.	Walk 110 yds.	2 times	3 or 4
(2) Joggers half mile in 10 to 12 minutes; walk and repeat.			
(3) Jog 110 yds.	Walk 110 yds.	2 times	3 or 4

Thursday 5 to 10 minute walk; easy stretching exercises

Friday (total distance: 1½ miles)			
(1) Jog 110 yds.	Walk 110 yds.	2 times	3 or 4
(2) Jog 330 yds.	Walk 110 yds.		3 or 4
(3) Slow fartlek jog for 4 to 6 minutes.			
(4) Jog 110 yds.	Walk 110 yds.	2 times	3 or 4

Saturday Consider optional program today or tomorrow—not both

Sunday Optional program or 10 minute walk; stretching exercises

WALKER-JOGGER

The walker-jogger is the fellow who can't jog even with the best of intentions and the doctor's permission. At the first workout, he finds he can't move faster than a walk. The reasons usually are weakness from prolonged illness or injury, or too many years of the good life.

For example, one man in his mid-50's found that even slow running aggravated an old football injury and caused swelling of one knee. The pain took most of the pleasure from the exercise.

For such conditions, the walker-jogger program will help. The principle is the same as regular jogging. The walker works out on a schedule. He starts slowly, gradually increasing the distance and the pace. He walks then rests. The goal is extended comfortable walking that puts gradual stress on the heart, lungs and muscles. The walking program has the flexibility of the regular program. The walker-jogger increases or decreases his program according to his ability. As his fitness improves, his heart, lungs and muscles improve their efficiency. He trains himself up to where he can enter the regular program.

First Week—Suggested Monday, Wednesday and Friday

Walk 55 yards	Rest 30 to 60 seconds	4 times
Walk 110 yards	Rest 1 to 2 minutes	2 times
Walk 55 yards	Rest 30 to 60 seconds	2 times

Second Week

Walk 55 yards	Rest 30 to 60 seconds	4 times
Walk 220 yards	Rest 1 to 2 minutes	2 times
Walk 55 yards	Rest 30 to 60 seconds	2 times

Third Week

Walk 55 yards	Rest 30 to 60 seconds	4 times
Walk 440 yards	Rest 1 to 2 minutes	2 times
Walk 110 yards	Rest 1 to 2 minutes	2 times
Walk 55 yards	Rest 30 to 60 seconds	2 times

Fourth Week

Walk 55 yards	Rest 30 to 60 seconds	4 times
Walk 220 yards	Rest 1 to 2 minutes	2 times
Walk 110 yards	Rest 1 to 2 minutes	4 times
Walk 55 yards	Rest 30 to 60 seconds	4 times

11

Plan B

SCHEDULE FOR MEN AND WOMEN IN AVERAGE CONDITION

Who Uses Plan B

More joggers begin with Plan B than Plans A and C simply because more are in average condition. About 80 percent of the men and 60 percent of the women will begin with this conditioning plan.

The man or woman who is a typical Plan B jogger plays an occasional game of golf, mows the lawn, does some gardening and the usual household chores. He is from 10 to 15 percent overweight and tires quickly when he does more than usual.

To improve fitness, he needs the limited structure and the training principles of Plan B. They are geared to his present level of fitness.

Week I

The distance is 1 mile for each workout.

If the schedule for the first day seems too long, jog only as much of the schedule as is comfortable. Gradually increase the distance until you can do the first schedule without strain, then follow the regular plan.

If, after two or three workouts, you still have difficulty, then you may have overrated your level of fitness. Consider Plan A for a few weeks. The schedules are arranged so that if you improve quickly, you can easily return to Plan B.

Here are some points to keep in mind as you begin your first Plan B workout:

1. Although the schedules are arranged for Monday, Wednesday and Friday, the days are not compulsory. Use Tuesday, Thursday and Saturday if you wish. Just remember the "hard-easy" principle: exercise one day, rest the next.

2. Start at a moderate speed. Almost without exception, joggers begin by running too fast. They develop sore muscles the next day. Jogging for beginners is slow, just faster than a walk.

3. To find the right beginning pace, try the "talk test." If jogging the first 55 or 110 yards leaves you gasping and too winded to talk with your companions, you're going too fast. Slow down and walk.

4. Mark your performance on the Progress Chart.

5. The idea is to finish your workout exhilarated, not exhausted.

TRAIN, DON'T STRAIN

Week I

ace 1 = 110 yds. at 55 to 60 seconds, or 55 yds. at 25 to 30 econds

Ionday
total distance: 1 mile)

				Pace
(1)	Jog 55 yds.	Walk 55 yds.	4 times	1
(2)	Jog 110 yds.	Walk 110 yds.	4 times	1
(3)	Jog 55 yds.	Walk 55 yds.	4 times	1

uesday 5 or 10 minute walk; easy stretching exercises

/ednesday
total distance: 1 mile)

				Pace
(1)	Jog 55 yds.	Walk 55 yds.	3 times	1
(2)	Jog 110 yds.	Walk 110 yds.	5 times	1
(3)	Jog 55 yds.	Walk 55 yds.	3 times	1

hursday 5 or 10 minute walk; easy stretching exercises

riday
total distance: 1 mile)

				Pace
(1)	Jog 55 yds.	Walk 55 yds.	2 times	1
(2)	Jog 110 yds.	Walk 110 yds.	6 times	1
(3)	Jog 55 yds.	Walk 55 yds.	2 times	1

aturday 5 to 10 minute walk; change the scenery

unday 5 to 10 minute walk; easy stretching exercises

Week II

The distance is 1 mile for each workout. The pace is moderate.

As mentioned, your schedule is a scaled-down version of a training pattern that has produced thousands of contented joggers as well as a long list of international and national track and field champions at the University of Oregon.

As part of the pattern for both joggers and runners, the schedules are arranged so the distance and pace are increased by plan. In Plan B, your distance and pace will increase every two weeks until at 12 weeks you will comfortably jog 2½ miles.

1. If you find the schedule too strenuous and develop aches and pains and sore joints, don't lay off. The problem will just recur. Rather, cut down on the distance or the speed. Running on a soft surface will help relieve the aches and pains. (See Reconditioning, page 37.)

2. Another possible pain is muscle cramps or spasms. You may need more salt. Take some unless you have been specifically advised not to take salt. A cup of bouillon 30 minutes before a meal can be helpful. It supplies salt and takes the edge off the appetite.

3. If after cutting down the distance and speed, you still find the schedule too strenuous, *walk through the exercises.* At the end of the second week's schedule, take your psychological pulse. Be honest with yourself. Should you stay with *Plan B* or drop back to *Plan A?*

TRAIN, DON'T STRAIN

Week II

Pace 1 = 110 yds. at 55 to 60 seconds, or 25 to 30 seconds for 55 yds.
Pace 2 = 110 yds. at 45 to 50 seconds, or 20 to 25 seconds for 55 yds.

Monday
(total distance: 1¼ miles)

				Pace
(1)	Jog 55 yds.	Walk 55 yds.	4 times	1 or 2
(2)	Jog 110 yds.	Walk 110 yds.	2 times	1 or 2
(3)	Jog 220 yds.	Walk 220 yds.	2 times	1 or 2
(4)	Jog 110 yds.	Walk 110 yds.	2 times	1 or 2

Tuesday 5 or 10 minute walk; easy stretching exercises

Wednesday
(total distance: 1¼ miles)

(1) To establish pace, jog 110 yds. at about 56 seconds. This is 4 miles per hour. See how long you can jog continuously with comfort (steady fartlek). Walk to recover. Take another continuous jog, then walk. Repeat as needed.

Thursday 5 or 10 minute walk; easy stretching exercises

Friday
(total distance: 1¼ miles)

				Pace
(1)	Jog 110 yds.	Walk 110 yds.	4 times	2
(2)	Jog steadily 330 yds. (330 yds. in about 2 minutes, 48 seconds). Walk as needed to recover.			1
(3)	Jog 110 yds.	Walk 110 yds.	4 times	2

Saturday 5 to 10 minute walk; change the scenery

Sunday 5 to 10 minute walk; easy stretching exercises

Week III

The distance is 1½ miles. The pace increases.

1. Oregon runners and joggers use another device as part of their training plan. They carry out specific kinds of exercises on given days. For example, both you and the runners have three workouts each week and each day will have a specified kind of exercise:

   a. On Monday, you will do *only* interval work (alternate jogging and walking at different distances).

   b. On Wednesday, you will do New Zealand fartlek (slow steady jogging).

   c. On Friday, you will do a combination of interval and fartlek jogging. You will follow this routine in all your workouts for the next 10 weeks.

2. You have your first try at New Zealand fartlek on Wednesday. This is slow *steady* jogging for as long as you comfortably can. With steady jogging, the pace is quite slow, probably slower than you think you should run. Certainly slower than the pace you use for interval jogging. Use the "talk test" to check your pace.

3. *Optional Program*: Your fitness has improved over the past three weeks. You can now consider an optional program designed to increase gradually your total distance each week. On Saturday or Sunday, not both, take a long walk or do some slow jogging and walking for a mile or two. Change the scenery. Make it a holiday.

   Don't forget the walking and stretching on Tuesday and Thursday.

TRAIN, DON'T STRAIN

Week III

Pace 1 = 110 yds. at 55 to 60 seconds
Pace 2 = 110 yds. at 45 to 50 seconds
Pace 3 = 110 yds. at 35 to 40 seconds

				Pace
Monday				
(total distance: 1½ miles)				
(1)	Jog 110 yds.	Walk 110 yds.	4 times	3
(2)	Jog 220 yds.	Walk 220 yds.	2 times	3
(3)	Jog 330 yds.	Walk 330 yds.		3
(4)	Jog 110 yds.	Walk 110 yds.		2 or 3

Tuesday 5 or 10 minute walk; easy stretching exercises

Wednesday				
(total distance: 1½ miles)				
(1)	Jog 110 yds.	Walk 110 yds.	4 times	2 or 3
(2)	Slow, steady jogging. Walk as needed. Then resume the slow, steady continuous jogging. 1 mile.			1 or 2

Thursday 5 or 10 minute walk; easy stretching exercises

Friday				
(total distance: 1½ miles)				
(1)	Jog 110 yds.	Walk 110 yds.		3
(2)	Jog 330 yds.	Walk 330 yds.		3
(3)	Jog 220 yds.	Walk 220 yds.		3
(4)	A slow continuous jog for 440 yds. Walk as needed.			1
(5)	Jog 110 yds.	Walk 110 yds.	4 times	2

Saturday Consider optional program today or tomorrow—not both

Sunday Optional program or 10 minute walk; stretching exercises

Week IV

The distance is $1\frac{1}{2}$ miles.

The schedule is quite similar to last week's: interval work the first day, New Zealand fartlek the second, and a combination of interval and fartlek on the third day.

How is your technique? Easy and natural? If not, perhaps you should reread the paragraphs on "How to Jog."

Mark your performance on the Progress Chart.

TRAIN, DON'T STRAIN

Week IV

Pace 1 = 110 yds. at 55 to 60 seconds
Pace 2 = 110 yds. at 45 to 50 seconds
Pace 3 = 110 yds. at 35 to 40 seconds

				Pace
Monday (total distance: 1½ miles)				
(1)	Jog 110 yds.	Walk 110 yds.		2 or 3
(2)	Jog 220 yds.	Walk 220 yds.		2 or 3
(3)	Jog 110 yds.	Walk 110 yds.		2 or 3
(4)	Jog continuously for ¾ mile. Walk as needed.			1
(5)	Jog 110 yds.	Walk 110 yds.		2 or 3

Tuesday 5 or 10 minute walk; easy stretching exercises

Wednesday (total distance: 1½ miles)				
(1)	Jog continuously (steady fartlek). Walk at intervals as needed.			1 or 2

Thursday 5 or 10 minute walk; easy stretching exercises

Friday (total distance: 1½ miles)				
(1)	Jog 110 yds.	Walk 110 yds.		2 or 3
(2)	Jog 330 yds.	Walk 330 yds.		2 or 3
(3)	Slow, steady jogging, 880 yds. Walk as needed.			1
(4)	Jog 110 yds.	Walk 110 yds.	3 times	2 or 3

Saturday Consider optional program today or tomorrow—not both

Sunday Optional program or 10 minute walk; stretching exercises

Week V

The distance is 1¾ miles.

In the training of Oregon runners, distances and pace are increased every two weeks, provided the runner can handle it.

Your jogging schedule also calls for increased distance and pace every two weeks, providing you can handle it. Anytime you feel you can't handle a new pace or distance, stay on the present schedule until you feel you can. Make haste slowly.

Any aches and pains? For relief, see the Reconditioning Plan, page 37.

TRAIN, DON'T STRAIN

Week V

Pace 1 = 110 yds. at 55 to 60 seconds
Pace 2 = 110 yds. at 45 to 50 seconds
Pace 3 = 110 yds. at 35 to 40 seconds

				Pace
Monday (total distance: 1¾ miles)				
(1)	Jog 110 yds.	Walk 110 yds.	4 times	2 or 3
(2)	Jog 330 yds.	Walk 330 yds.		2 or 3
(3)	Jog 220 yds.	Walk 220 yds.	2 times	2 or 3
(4)	Jog 110 yds.	Walk 110 yds.	3 times	2 or 3

Tuesday 5 to 10 minute walk; easy stretching exercises

Wednesday
(total distance: 1¾ miles)
(1) Jog continuously (steady fartlek). Walk as needed. 2 or 3

Thursday 5 to 10 minute walk; easy stretching exercises

Friday (total distance: 1¾ miles)				
(1)	Jog 330 yds.	Walk 330 yds.		2 or 3
(2)	Jog 220 yds.	Walk 220 yds.	2 times	2 or 3
(3)	Jog 110 yds.	Walk 110 yds.	2 times	2 or 3
(4)	Steady fartlek for 1100 yds. (⅝ mile).			1 or 2

Saturday Consider optional program today or tomorrow—not both

Sunday Optional program or 10 minute walk; stretching exercises

Week VI

The distance is $1\frac{3}{4}$ miles.

This week you do two new things: (1) You use Swedish fartlek, and (2) you run a jogger's mile.

Swedish fartlek is an exercise used to break routine and add extra enjoyment to the workout. Fartlek, a Swedish word, literally translates as "speed play." The implication is that you can play, fool around, in this workout.

In a Swedish fartlek workout, runners apply all the elements of a race. They use short quick bursts as though to pass or catch another runner; they coast; they slow down, then speed up again, always changing the cadence. In training, a four-minute miler may do this for as long as an hour.

You will use Swedish fartlek on the second day of the schedule, doing all the things that runners do, plus walking. If Swedish fartlek proves too difficult, slow down and return to the slow, steady New Zealand fartlek.

On the third day, you will get a chance to test your judgment of pace by running a "jogger's mile." A "jogger's mile" is not a competitive event where you set out to beat another jogger. Rather, it is an exercise that lets you test your progress toward that elusive goal, physical fitness. Each jogger picks a time and sees how close he comes to matching it. A 15- or 12-minute mile pace is about right. Certainly, at this stage, you should never run faster than 10 minutes per mile.

TRAIN, DON'T STRAIN

Week VI

Pace 2 = 110 yds. at 45 to 50 seconds
Pace 3 = 110 yds. at 35 to 40 seconds
Pace 4 = 110 yds. at 25 to 30 seconds

Monday
(total distance: 1¾ miles)

				Pace
(1)	Jog 110 yds.	Walk 110 yds.	4 times	2, 3 or 4
(2)	Jog 330 yds.	Walk 330 yds.		2, 3 or 4
(3)	Jog 220 yds.	Walk 220 yds.	2 times	2, 3 or 4
(4)	Jog 110 yds.	Walk 110 yds.	3 times	2, 3 or 4

Tuesday 5 to 10 minute walk; easy stretching exercises

Wednesday
(total distance: 1¾ miles)

(1) Continuous jogging for 1¾ miles. Vary the pace from fast to a very slow jog (varied fartlek).

Thursday 5 to 10 minute walk; easy stretching exercises

Friday
(total distance: 1¾ miles)

(1) Jog a mile at a predetermined pace (a jogger's mile) in about 10, 12 or 15 minutes.

(2)	Jog 220 yds.	Walk 220 yds.	2 times	2, 3 or 4
(3)	Jog 110 yds.	Walk 110 yds.	4 times	2, 3 or 4

Saturday Consider optional program today or tomorrow—not both

Sunday Optional program or 10 minute walk; stretching exercises

Week VII

The distance is 2 miles. The pace is quicker.

You have continued variety in the workout. On the second day, you can choose between New Zealand and Swedish fartlek.

Does Plan B provide enough challenge? Look at the Plan C schedule for 2 miles. Perhaps it is better suited for your present needs.

Don't forget the Optional Program on Saturday or Sunday. Take a good jog or walk. Change the scenery. Enjoy yourself.

Check the Progress Chart.

TRAIN, DON'T STRAIN

Week VII

Pace 2 = 110 yds. at 45 to 50 seconds
Pace 3 = 110 yds. at 35 to 40 seconds
Pace 4 = 110 yds. at 25 to 30 seconds

Monday
(total distance: 2 miles)

			Pace
(1)	Jog 110 yds. Walk 110 yds.	3 times	3 or 4
(2)	Jog 330 yds. Walk as needed. Try 110 yds.	2 times	3 or 4
(3)	Jog 220 yds. Walk as needed. Try 110 yds.	4 times	3 or 4
(4)	Jog 110 yds. Walk 110 yds.	3 times	3 or 4

Tuesday 5 or 10 minute walk; easy stretching exercises

Wednesday
(total distance: 2 miles)
(1) Either a slow steady jog (steady fartlek) or a varied pace (varied fartlek) for 2 miles. Walk as needed.

Thursday 5 or 10 minute walk; easy stretching exercises

Friday
(total distance: 2 miles)

		Pace
(1)	110-440-330-110-yd. jogs. Walk as needed after each.	3 or 4
(2)	Slow steady jog for 1½ miles. Walk as needed.	2 or 3

Saturday Consider optional program today or tomorrow—not both

Sunday Optional program or 10 minute walk; stretching exercises

Week VIII

The distance is 2 miles.

Here's more strategy from the Oregon plan for training runners:

1. A training race is scheduled every two or three weeks.

2. In a training race, the runner never runs at full speed. Instead, with the coach, he selects a pace of approximately ¾ of his capability.

You will use the same strategy and test yourself every two or three weeks with a "jogger's mile." In all your training you *never* run at full speed. In a "jogger's mile," you will move along at a comfortable pace. Use the "talk test" to gauge pace.

You've been at it now for eight weeks. How about trying something new? This Saturday or Sunday try a little cross-country running over some hills. It's a wonderful change of pace. But don't blithely attack a hill. Go at it slowly. Running up a hill requires a tremendous amount of energy. It also brings into play some muscles you haven't been using while running in the flat. In the training of track men, running the hills is used to build strength and endurance. It also gets them away from the sometimes tedious routine of circling a track.

Running in the hills will do much the same for you. It will build strength and get you away from your regular routine.

One caution: you can legitimately expect some stiff and sore muscles for a day or two after hill running for the first time. The best medicine is to go right on with your jogging schedule. It's nothing serious. Be glad you found those muscles and they still work. If the aches and pains persist, see the Reconditioning Plan, page 37.

TRAIN, DON'T STRAIN

Week VIII

Pace 1 = 110 yds. at 55 to 60 seconds
Pace 2 = 110 yds. at 45 to 50 seconds
Pace 3 = 110 yds. at 35 to 40 seconds
Pace 4 = 110 yds. at 25 to 30 seconds

			Pace
Monday			
(total distance: 2 miles)			
(1) Jog 110 yds.	Walk 110 yds.	4 times	3 or 4
(2) Jog 220 yds.	Walk 110 yds.	2 times	3 or 4
(3) Jog 330 yds.	Walk 110 yds.	2 times	3 or 4
(4) Jog 220 yds.	Walk 110 yds.	3 times	3 or 4

Tuesday 5 to 10 minute walk; easy stretching exercises

Wednesday
(total distance: 2 miles)

(1) Jog 110 yds.	Walk 110 yds.	2 times	2
(2) Slow steady fartlek for 1½ to 1¾ miles. Walk as needed.			1 or 2

Thursday 5 to 10 minute walk; easy stretching exercises

Friday
(total distance: 2 miles)

(1) A jogger's mile. Declare your pace.			
(2) Jog 220 yds.	Walk 220 yds.	3 times	3 or 4
(3) 440 yds. at a slow jog.			1 or 2

Saturday Consider optional program either today or tomorrow—not both

Sunday Optional program or 10 minute walk; stretching exercises

Week IX

The distance is 2 miles.

Joggers get their first big charge from improved fitness at about six weeks. At nine weeks the feeling of well-being grows.

Look at the pace chart. You are now jogging 220 yards in close to 60 seconds. You started at about 90 seconds. You have advanced tremendously. Your heart is working more efficiently, the tone and elasticity of your entire cardiovascular system are up and your lungs now handle a greater volume of oxygen. Congratulations.

Check the Progress Chart.

TRAIN, DON'T STRAIN

Week IX

Pace 3 = 110 yds. at 35 to 40 seconds
Pace 4 = 110 yds. at 25 to 30 seconds

			Pace
Monday			
(total distance: 2 miles)			
(1) Jog 330-220-110 yds. Walk as needed to recover between jogs.		2 times	3 or 4
(2) Jog 220 yds.	Walk as needed.	4 times	3 or 4
(3) Jog 110 yds.	Walk as needed.	2 times	3 or 4

Tuesday 5 or 10 minute walk; easy stretching exercises

Wednesday			
(total distance: 2 miles)			
(1) A varied fartlek for about 1½ miles. Walk as needed.			
(2) Jog 110 yds.	Walk as needed between jogs.	5 times	3 or 4

Thursday 5 or 10 minute walk; easy stretching exercises

Friday			
(total distance: 2 miles)			
(1) Jog 220 yds.	Walk as needed between jogs.	2 times	3 or 4
(2) Jog 440 yds.	Walk as needed between jogs.	2 times	3 or 4
(3) Slow, steady fartlek for ½ mile.			1 or 2
(4) Jog 110 yds.	Walk 110 yds.	2 times	2 or 3

Saturday Consider optional program today or tomorrow—not both

Sunday Optional program or 10 minute walk; stretching exercises

Week X

The distance is $2\frac{1}{2}$ miles.

In the Oregon plan, as you come to the last weeks of training the schedules settle at a plateau. The distance remains the same each week. Only the pace changes.

The reason is that you are reaching the ceiling of your ability in this schedule. Remaining at the same distance for a couple of weeks helps you build a tolerance while you decide whether you wish to remain at this level of fitness, move ahead or drop back.

You'll make the decision in two more weeks.

Remember the walking and stretching on non-jogging days.

TRAIN, DON'T STRAIN

Week X

Pace 1 = 110 yds. at 55 to 60 seconds
Pace 2 = 110 yds. at 45 to 50 seconds
Pace 3 = 110 yds. at 35 to 40 seconds
Pace 4 = 110 yds. at 25 to 30 seconds

Monday
(total distance: 2½ miles)

			Pace
(1) Jog 110 yds.	Walk as needed between jogs.	2 times	3 or 4
(2) Jog 660 yds.	Walk as needed between jogs.		3 or 4
(3) Jog 440 yds.	Walk as needed between jogs.	2 times	3 or 4
(4) Jog 330 yds.	Walk as needed between jogs.	4 times	3 or 4

Tuesday 5 or 10 minute walk; easy stretching exercises

Wednesday
(total distance: 2½ miles)
(1) Varied fartlek. Walk as needed.

Thursday 5 or 10 minute walk; easy stretching exercises

Friday
(total distance: 2½ miles)

(1) A jogger's mile at a declared pace. Walk as needed to recover after mile finished.	2, 3 or 4
(2) Steady fartlek about 1¼ miles. Walk as needed.	1 or 2

Saturday Consider optional program today or tomorrow—not both

Sunday Optional program or 10 minute walk; stretching exercises

Week XI

The distance is $2\frac{1}{2}$ miles.

Some joggers over estimate their physical ability. If you find the increased pace too great, the routine too strenuous, *drop back two weeks.*

Remember the Optional Plan on Saturday or Sunday.

Check the Progress Chart.

TRAIN, DON'T STRAIN

Week XI

Pace 2 = 110 yds. at 45 to 50 seconds
Pace 3 = 110 yds. at 35 to 40 seconds
Pace 4 = 110 yds. at 25 to 30 seconds

			Pace
Monday (total distance: 2½ miles)			
(1) Jog 110 yds.	Walk as needed between jogs.	4 times	2, 3 or 4
(2) Jog 440 yds.	Walk as needed between jogs.	2 times	2, 3 or 4
(3) Jog 330 yds.	Walk as needed between jogs.	2 times	2, 3 or 4
(4) Jog 220 yds.	Walk as needed between jogs.	4 times	2, 3 or 4
(5) Jog 110 yds.	Walk as needed. between jogs.	4 times	2, 3 or 4

Tuesday 5 or 10 minute walk; easy stretching exercises

Wednesday
(total distance: 2½ miles)
(1) Varied fartlek. Walk as needed.

Thursday 5 or 10 minute walk; easy stretching exercises

Friday
(total distance: 2½ miles)

(1) A jogger's mile at a selected pace. Walk as needed to recover.			2, 3 or 4
(2) Jog 440 yds.	Walk as needed between jogs.	2 times	4
(3) Jog 330 yds.	Walk as needed between jogs.	2 times	4
(4) Jog 220 yds.	Walk as needed between jogs.	2 times	4

Saturday Consider optional program today or tomorrow—not both

Sunday Optional program or 10 minute walk; stretching exercises

Week XII

The distance is 2½ miles.

This is the last week of Plan B. Congratulations on coming this far. If you're a typical jogger, you've now trained yourself up to a level of fitness you thought you'd lost forever.

Now you've got three ways to go. You can move up to the more permissive exercises of Plan C and work toward a still higher level of fitness. Or, you can maintain your present level, or even drop back.

You are the best judge of what level is best for you.

Any way you go, you have a wonderful start in developing a *habit of permanent moderate exercise.* No matter what kind of setback you experience, you can always recondition yourself through the flexible jogging program.

Week XII

Pace 2 = 110 yds. at 45 to 55 seconds
Pace 3 = 110 yds. at 35 to 40 seconds
Pace 4 = 110 yds. at 25 to 30 seconds
Pace 5 = 110 yds. at 20 to 25 seconds

			Pace
Monday (total distance: 2½ miles)			
(1) Jog 110 yds.	Walk as needed between jogs.	2 times	3, 4 or 5
(2) Jog 440 yds.	Walk as needed between jogs.	3 times	3, 4 or 5
(3) Jog 330 yds.	Walk as needed between jogs.	3 times	3, 4 or 5
(4) Jog 220 yds.	Walk as needed between jogs.	3 times	3, 4 or 5

Tuesday 5 or 10 minute walk; easy stretching exercises

Wednesday
(total distance: 2½ miles)

(1) Steady fartlek.	1, 2 or 3

Thursday 5 or 10 minute walk; easy stretching exercises

Friday
(total distance: 2½ miles)

(1) A jogger's mile at a declared pace.	2, 3 or 4
(2) A mile of interval distances of your choice.	2, 3 or 4
(3) Varied fartlek for ½ mile.	1, 2, 3, 4

Saturday Consider optional program today or tomorrow—not both

Sunday Optional program or 10 minute walk; stretching exercises

12

Plan C

FOR MEN AND WOMEN OF BETTER THAN AVERAGE PHYSICAL CONDITION

Plan C is more permissive than the other plans. It is designec especially for active men and women who will reconditioi quickly. Experience shows that this group does not need th limited structure of Plans A and B. Plan C joggers are an activ group. They hunt, fish, ski and engage in strenuous outdoo sports. Basically, they are in better than average physical con dition. By following Plan C, they will be able to do all thes things with increased vigor and confidence.

TRUST YOUR INSTINCTS

ᵓerhaps you are already running regularly. Keep it up. Your ɩatural instincts probably have directed you to the right pro- ɟram for your needs.

Still, the training principles in this book may offer something ·ou have been missing. Try gradually working them into your wn schedule.

For example, if you've been running on a track, in a gym or ome other fixed location, cut loose and run cross country. Or, you've been enjoying the freedom of cross-country, discipline ourself with a "measured mile."

One caution: in the excitement of trying something new, be areful not to increase or decrease the distance and the pace ɔo greatly. You might wake up stiff and sore, or you might find ıe schedule too easy and lose interest.

If aches and pains do develop from the new schedule, follow ıe instructions under "Reconditioning," page 37.

HOW TO MIX YOUR SCHEDULE WITH THE JOGGING SCHEDULE

you haven't been working out by a fixed schedule, one way measure progress is by how you feel. A more helpful way is write out what you intend to do each day for a week ahead. you don't know exactly how far you've been running, make ı approximation. Then consider this plan:

1. Run two days of the week exactly as usual.
2. On the other day, cover the same distance but in a different ıttern. Do intervals if you've been running cross-country; cross- ɔuntry if you've been doing intervals.
3. Don't increase or decrease the distance more than ½ mile a mile each week of a two week period.
4. If you've been running every day and want to test the fectiveness of the every-other-day pattern (hard-easy princi- e), move gradually into the routine. Take several days to make e transfer, shortening the amount of exercise on the light days ıd lengthening it on strenuous days.

Week I

Each workout this week covers a mile. Although you're fit and probably can do more, the distance is purposely short. If you already are regularly running beyond this distance, give the shorter distance a try just to acquaint yourself with the principles. But before you end the workout, finish your regular schedule with a "free run."

A quick review will help:

1. The schedules work on the "hard-easy" principle. Work hard one day, do less the following day. Daily workouts are not recommended. Experience has shown that joggers and runners, including world champions, who train vigorously every day develop chronic fatigue.

2. There are a minimum of three hard days in each week:

a. On Monday, you do *only* interval work (alternate jogging and walking at different distances).

b. On Wednesday, you do New Zealand fartlek (slow, steady jogging) or Swedish fartlek (change of pace jogging—slow down, speed up, coast, quick bursts and periods of steady jogging).

c. On Friday, you do a combination of interval and fartlek jogging.

3. Although you can jog at a more rapid pace than Plan A and B joggers, test your pace the same as they do. Try the "talk test." If jogging the first 55 or 110 yards leaves you gasping and too breathless to talk with your companions, you're going too fast. Slow down or walk. Train, don't strain.

4. The schedules are arranged for Monday, Wednesday and Friday, but these days are not compulsory. Use Tuesday, Thursday and Saturday if you wish. Just remember the "hard-easy" principle: hard one day, easy the next.

5. For a more complete rundown on the principles of jogging and other details, take a few minutes and read through the instructions in Plan B.

6. Remember to mark your performance on the Progress Chart.

Week I

Pace 1 = 110 yds. at 55 to 60 seconds, or 55 yds. at 25 to 30 seconds
Pace 2 = 110 yds. at 45 to 50 seconds
Pace 3 = 110 yds. at 35 to 40 seconds

				Pace
Monday				
(total distance: 1¼ miles)				
(1)	Jog 55 yds.	Walk 55 yds.	4 times	2
(2)	Jog 110 yds.	Walk 110 yds.	4 times	2
(3)	Jog 55 yds.	Walk 55 yds.	4 times	2

Tuesday An easy day. Take a walk. Easy stretching exercises.

Wednesday
(total distance: 1¼ miles)

(1)	Jog 55 yds.	Walk 55 yds.	4 times	2
(2)	New Zealand fartlek or *slow, steady* jogging. Jog for as long as comfortable. (Pace 1 is 4 miles per hour, a quick walking pace.)			
(3)	Jog 55 yds.	Walk 55 yds.	4 times	2

Thursday Walk. Stretch and pick flowers.

Friday
(total distance: 1¼ miles)

(1)	Jog 55 yds.	Walk 55 yds.	3 times	2
(2)	Jog 110 yds.	Walk 110 yds.	3 times	1
(3)	*Slow, steady* jog for 2 to 3 minutes.			
(4)	Jog 55 yds.	Walk 55 yds.	4 times	2 or 3

Saturday 5 to 10 minute walk; change the scenery

Sunday 5 to 10 minute walk; easy stretching exercises

Week II

The distance is $1\frac{1}{4}$ miles. If you found the first week too easy, you have at least two choices: (1) Use the permissive guide and add 25 to 50 percent to each part of each schedule. For example, jog 55 yards six times instead of four. Do three 110's instead of two. When you add distance, be sure to write it on your performance chart, so you will have a record. Or, (2) select a distance more suited to your needs and capability. Look at the sixth and eighth weeks for guides.

Optional program: Because you are in better than average condition, you can consider an optional program designed to increase your total distance each week. On Saturday or Sunday, not both, change the scenery. Take a long, slow jog or walk for about two to four miles. Go to the park or beach. Make it a holiday. Train, don't strain.

Week II

Pace 1 = 110 yds. at 55 to 60 seconds, or 55 yds. at 25 to 30 seconds
Pace 2 = 110 yds. at 45 to 50 seconds

				Pace
Monday				
(total distance: 1¼ miles)				
(1)	Jog 55 yds.	Walk 55 yds.	4 times	2
(2)	Jog 110 yds.	Walk 110 yds.	2 times	2
(3)	Jog 220 yds.	Walk 220 yds.	2 times	2
(4)	Jog 110 yds.	Walk 110 yds.	2 times	2

Tuesday Easy stretching. Walk.

Wednesday
(total distance: 1¼ miles)

(1)	Jog 55 yds.	Walk 55 yds.	2 times	2
(2)	Jog 110 yds.	Walk 110 yds.	2 times	2
(3)	New Zealand fartlek (steady) for several minutes			1
(4)	Jog 55 yds.	Walk 55 yds.	2 times	2

Thursday Stretching. Gardening. Walking.

Friday
(total distance: 1¼ miles)

(1)	Jog 55 yds.	Walk 55 yds.	4 times	2
(2)	New Zealand fartlek (steady) for several minutes			1
(3)	Jog 110 yds.	Walk 110 yds.	4 times	2

Saturday Consider optional program today or tomorrow—not both

Sunday Optional program or 20 minute walk; stretching exercises

Week III

The suggested minimum is 1½ miles and the maximum is 2 miles. To make up the half mile from 1½ to 2, you can either increase the number of intervals or the distance of the interval. For example, on Monday jog four 220's instead of two. The same on Friday. Or add the necessary 110's. Don't forget the walking and stretching exercises on easy days. Train, don't strain.

Week III

Pace 1 = 110 yds. at 55 to 60 seconds
Pace 2 = 110 yds. at 45 to 50 seconds
Pace 3 = 110 yds. at 35 to 40 seconds

Monday
(total distance: 1½ to 2 miles)

				Pace
(1)	Jog 110 yds.	Walk 110 yds.	4 times	2
(2)	Jog 220 yds.	Walk 110 yds.	2 to 4 times	2
(3)	Jog 110 yds.	Walk 110 yds.	2 times	2

Tuesday Easy stretching and walking.

Wednesday
(total distance: 1½ to 2 miles)

				Pace
(1)	Jog 110 yds.	Walk 110 yds.	4 times	2 or 3
(2)	*Slow, steady* jogging. Walk as needed, then resume the slow continuous jogging.			1 or 2

Thursday Walk. Watch the girls. Stretch.

Friday
(total distance: 1½ to 2 miles)

				Pace
(1)	Jog 110 yds.	Walk 110 yds.		3
(2)	Jog 220 yds.	Walk 110 yds.	2 to 4 times	3
(3)	Jog 330 yds.	Walk 110 yds.		3
(4)	Jog continuously, walking if needed.			1
(5)	Jog 110 yds.	Walk 110 yds.	4 times	2 or 3

Saturday Consider optional program today or tomorrow—not both

Sunday Optional program or 30 minute walk; stretching exercises

Week IV

The distance is 1¾ to 2 miles. Again, the schedule is permissive. Add the distance if you feel you need it. Don't overdo. There is a "best" distance for your present fitness.

You should finish your workout exhilarated, not exhausted. If you had little sleep last night, or an extra tough day at home or in the office, take that into consideration and do less. Train, don't strain.

HOW ABOUT A RUN IN THE HILLS?

A good test of growing fitness is to jog up, over and down some hills. But don't blithely attack a hill. Running up a hill requires a tremendous amount of energy. It also brings into play some new muscles. If there are no hills close to home, save the hill running for Saturday or Sunday. If you want to make hill running part of the regular schedule, get at the hill early in the workout. Finishing a workout with a hill can take away some of the glow. (See page 31 for instructions for hill running.)

Week IV

ace 1 = 110 yds. at 55 to 60 seconds
ace 2 = 110 yds. at 45 to 50 seconds
ace 3 = 110 yds. at 35 to 40 seconds

onday
total distance: 1¾ to 2 miles)

				Pace
(1)	Jog 110 yds.	Walk 110 yds.	2 times	2 or 3
(2)	Jog 220 yds.	Walk 110 yds.	4 times	2 or 3
(3)	Jog 330 yds.	Walk 110 yds.		2 or 3
(4)	Jog 110 yds.	Walk 110 yds.	2 times	2 or 3

uesday Easy stretching and walking.

Vednesday
total distance: 1¾ to 2 miles)

(1)	Jog continuously (steady fartlek); walk as needed for 1¾ to 2 miles.	1 or 2

hursday Walk. Watch the girls. Stretch.

riday
total distance: 1¾ to 2 miles)

(1)	Jog 110 yds.	Walk 110 yds.	2 times	2 or 3
(2)	Jog 330 yds.	Walk 110 yds.	2 times	2 or 3
(3)	Slow steady jogging for 880 yds. or more.			1 or 2
(4)	Jog 110 yds.	Walk 110 yds.	4 times	2 or 3

aturday Consider optional program today or tomorrow—not both

unday Optional program or 30 minute walk; stretching exercises

Week V

The distance is 2 to 3 miles. The schedule is permissive. If yo have confined yourself to a track, park, backyard or some fixe location, try the freedom of running in the street or road. Chang the scenery.

Don't run a red light, and watch out for vicious dogs. If ache and pains develop, don't stop. See page 37 for reconditionin instructions.

Remember the Performance Chart.

Week V

Pace 1 = 110 yds. at 55 to 60 seconds
Pace 2 = 110 yds. at 45 to 50 seconds
Pace 3 = 110 yds. at 35 to 40 seconds

Pace

Monday
(total distance: 2 to 3 miles)

				Pace
(1)	Jog 110 yds.	Walk 110 yds.	2 to 4 times	3
(2)	Jog 440 yds.	Walk 110 yds.	2 to 3 times	3
(3)	Jog 330-220-110 yds.	Walk 110 yds. after each.	2 to 3 times	3

Tuesday Walk to a different neighborhood—stretching.

Wednesday
(total distance: 2 to 3 miles)

				Pace
(1)	Jog 110 yds.	Walk 110 yds.	2 times	3
(2)	Steady fartlek. Walk as needed for 1½ to 2 miles.			2
(3)	Jog 110 yds.	Walk 110 yds.	2 times	3

Thursday Walking and stretching.

Friday
(total distance: 2¾ to 4 miles)

				Pace
(1)	Jog 110 yds.	Walk 110 yds.	6 times	3 or 4
(2)	Fartlek jog for a comfortable time.			2 or 3
(3)	Jog 330-220-110 yds.; walk 110 after each. Repeat as necessary to complete the day's distance.			

Saturday Consider optional program today or tomorrow—not both

Sunday Optional program or 30 minute walk; easy stretching

Week VI

The distance is 2 to 3 miles. For the past couple of weeks you'v been using the standard University of Oregon principle for train ing runners. If a runner can handle it, distance and pace are in creased every two weeks. *Your* pace and distance increase ever two weeks, providing you can handle it.

Don't forget the walking and stretching on easy days.

Think you might benefit from rereading the sections on tech nique—"How to Jog?"

Week VI

ace 2 = 110 yds. at 45 to 50 seconds
ace 3 = 110 yds. at 35 to 40 seconds
ace 4 = 110 yds. at 25 to 30 seconds

			Pace
Ionday			
total distance: 2 to 3 miles)			
(1) Jog 110 yds.	Walk 110 yds.	2 times	3 or 4
(2) Jog 440 yds.	Walk 110 yds.	2 times	3 or 4
(3) Jog 330-220-110 yds.	Walk 110 yds. after each.	2 times	3 or 4
(4) Jog 110 yds.	Walk 110 yds.		3 or 4

uesday Golf. Gardening. Walking.

'ednesday			
total distance: 2 to 3 miles)			
(1) Jog 110 yds.	Walk 110 yds.	4 times	3 or 4
(2) Jogger's mile in 10 or 12 minutes. Select your pace. Don't race!			
(3) Jog 110 yds.	Walk 110 yds.	4 times	3 or 4

hursday Walking and stretching.

riday
.otal distance: 2 to 3 miles)

(1) Jog 110 yds.	Walk 110 yds.	2 times	3 or 4
(2) Jog 330-220-110 yds. Walk 110 yds. after each.			3 or 4
(3) Steady fartlek jog until rest is needed.			2 or 3
(4) Jog 110 yds. Walk 110 yds. Repeat until your daily distance is completed. If you completed your distance in fartlek, skip this workout.			

turday Consider optional program today or tomorrow—not both

ınday Optional program or 30 minute walk; easy stretching

Week VII

For the next two weeks, the distance moves up again. It is now 2½ to 4 miles.

Would you like to test your judgment of pace? Try a jogger's mile. A "jogger's mile" is not a competitive event where you set out to beat another jogger. Rather, each jogger picks his own time and sees how close he can come to matching it.

When Plan B joggers try their first "jogger's mile," they are cautioned not to run faster than 10 minutes a mile. A 12- to 15-minute mile is even better. You are more fit and possibly can run faster. But remember, any time faster than seven minutes per mile is a run, not a jog. See the pace chart, page 41. Train, don't strain.

Week VII

'ace 2 = 110 yds. at 45 to 50 seconds
'ace 3 = 110 yds. at 35 to 40 seconds
'ace 4 = 110 yds. at 25 to 30 seconds

			Pace
Ionday			
total distance: 2½ to 4 miles)			
(1) Jog 110 yds.	Walk 110 yds.	2 times	3 or 4
(2) Jog 440 yds.	Walk 110 yds.	2 times	3 or 4
(3) Jog 330-220-110 yds.	Walk 110 yds. after each.	2 times	3 or 4
(4) Jog 110 yds.	Walk 110 yds.	2 times	3 or 4

'uesday Walk. Stretch.

Vednesday			
total distance: 2½ to 4 miles)			
(1) Jog 110 yds.	Walk 110 yds.	4 times	3 or 4
(2) A fartlek jog on varied terrain. Jog in a different location. Jog for 4 or 5 minutes or until you feel the need to rest. Repeat until you have completed the day's distance.			2 or 3

'hursday Walking. Storytelling. Stretching.

'riday			
total distance: 2½ to 4 miles)			
(1) Jog 110 yds.	Walk 110 yds.	2 times	3 or 4
(2) An easy fartlek jog for a comfortable distance.			2 or 3
(3) Jog 330-220-110 yds. Walk 110 yds. after each. Repeat until you complete the day's distance.			3 or 4

aturday Consider optional program today or tomorrow—not both

unday Optional program or 30 minute walk; easy stretching

Week VIII

The distance is 2¾ to 4 miles. Have you tried hill running yet? When you do, go at it slowly. You can legitimately expect some soreness from muscles you haven't used until now. Remember the walking and stretching exercises on easy days.

Don't forget to mark your performance on the Progress Chart.

Week VIII

Pace 2 = 110 yds. at 45 to 50 seconds
Pace 3 = 110 yds. at 35 to 40 seconds
Pace 4 = 110 yds. at 25 to 30 seconds

Monday
(total distance: 2¾ to 4 miles)

				Pace
(1)	Jog 110 yds.	Walk 110 yds.	2 times	3 or 4
(2)	Jog 440 yds.	Walk 110 yds.	4 times	3 or 4
(3)	Jog 330-220-110 yds. Walk 110 yds. after each.			3 or 4
(4)	Jog 110 yds.	Walk 110 yds.	3 times	3 or 4

Tuesday Walking and stretching.

Wednesday
(total distance: 2¾ to 4 miles)

				Pace
(1)	Jog 110 yds.	Walk 110 yds.	4 times	3 or 4
(2)	Jogger's mile. Pick your pace and see how steadily you can hold it. How close can you come?			
(3)	Fartlek jog at a very slow pace.			2 or 3
(4)	Jog 110 yds., walk 110 yds. as necessary to complete the day's distance.			3 or 4

Thursday Walking and stretching.

Friday
(total distance: 2 to 3 miles)

				Pace
(1)	Jog 110 yds.	Walk 110 yds.	2 times	3
(2)	Jog 440 yds.	Walk 110 yds.	2 times	3
(3)	Steady fartlek, walk as needed for ¾ mile.			2
(4)	Jog 110 yds.	Walk 110 yds.	3 times	3

Saturday Consider optional program today or tomorrow—not both

Sunday Optional program or 30 minute walk; stretching exercises

Week IX

The distance is 3 to 4 miles.

Joggers on Plans A and B will normally get their first big charge from improved fitness at about six weeks. At nine weeks the feeling of well-being grows. You too should feel the benefits of jogging about now, particularly if you have changed from a daily workout to an every-other-day schedule (hard-easy). The rest between workouts refreshes. The well conditioned runner learns early that rest is as important to his success as exercise.

Keep up the good work.

Week IX

Pace 3 = 110 yds. at 35 to 40 seconds
Pace 4 = 110 yds. at 25 to 30 seconds

Monday
(total distance: 3 to 4 miles)

				Pace
(1)	Jog 110 yds.	Walk 110 yds.	4 times	4
(2)	Jog 330-220-110 yds. Walk 110 yds. after each interval.		2 times	4
(3)	Jog 880 yds. (½ mile)		2 times	4
(4)	Jog 110 yds.	Walk 110 yds.	4 times	4

Tuesday Walking. Girl watching. Stretching.

Wednesday
(total distance: 3 to 4 miles)

(1)	Jog 110 yds.	Walk 110 yds.	4 times	4
(2)	A fartlek jog on varied terrain at varied pace (Swedish fartlek)			3
(3)	Jog 110 yds.; walk 110 yds. as needed if distance not completed in fartlek			

Thursday Walking and stretching.

Friday
(total distance: 3 to 4 miles)

(1)	Jog 110 yds.	Walk 110 yds.	4 times	4
(2)	Fartlek jog for ½ to ¾ mile			3
(3)	Jog 330-220-110; walk 110 yds. Repeat as necessary to complete day's distance			4

Saturday Consider optional program today or tomorrow—not both

Sunday Optional program or 30 minute walk; easy stretching

Week X

Distance is $3\frac{1}{2}$ to 5 miles.

One of the Oregon principles for training runners is to change from a two- to a three-week schedule in the final weeks of a regular training program. You are now in the last three weeks of this plan. You should begin to consider what to do about your permanent exercise habits. When you finish the plan, do you want to remain at this plateau, move ahead or drop back? The jogging plans are flexible and will fit *your* needs.

Have you taken up the optional program with a walk and jog on Saturday or Sunday? Let people stare. For some it's the only exercise.

Train, don't strain.

Week X

Pace 3 = 110 yds. at 35 to 40 seconds
Pace 4 = 110 yds. at 25 to 30 seconds

			Pace
Monday (total distance: 3½ to 5 miles)			
(1) Jog 110 yds.	Walk 110 yds.	4 times	4
(2) Jog 880 yds.	Walk 110 yds.	2 times	4
(3) Jog 330-220-110 yds.	Walk 110 yds. after each.	4 times	4
(4) Jog 110 yds.	Walk 110 yds.	2 times	4

Tuesday Walking and stretching

Wednesday (total distance: 3½ to 5 miles)			
(1) Jog 110 yds. Walk 110 yds. Select the pace you wish to maintain for a jogger's mile.			
(2) Jogger's mile at your selected pace.			
(3) Fartlek jog on varied terrain and at a varied comfortable pace to complete the distance.			3

Thursday Walking and stretching

Friday (total distance: 3½ to 5 miles)			
(1) Jog 110 yds.	Walk 110 yds.	4 times	4
(2) Slow, steady fartlek jog			3
(3) Jog 110 yds. Walk 110 yds. to complete the distance.			3 or 4

Saturday Consider optional program today or tomorrow—not both

Sunday Optional program or 30 minute walk; easy stretching

Week XI

The distance is 3¾ to 5 miles.

In establishing permanent exercise habits, do the activity you like. Run as fast or as far or as slow or as little as suits you. But, recognize that exercise is vital to your well-being. It is as important as eating. So bring them into balance. Exercise more and eat a bit less. No, eating while jogging is not the answer.

Week XI

Pace 3 = 110 yds. at 35 to 40 seconds
Pace 4 = 110 yds. at 25 to 30 seconds
Pace 5 = 110 yds. at 20 to 25 seconds

Monday
(total distance: 3¾ to 5 miles)

				Pace
(1)	Jog 110 yds.	Walk 110 yds.	4 times	4 or 5
(2)	Jog 880 yds.	Walk 110 yds.	2 times	4 or 5
(3)	Jog 330-220-110 yds. Walk 110 yds. after each.		2 times	4 or 5
(4)	Jog 110 yds.	Walk 110 yds.	4 times	4 or 5

Tuesday Walk. Pick flowers. Stretch.

Wednesday
(total distance: 3¾ to 5 miles)

(1)	Jog 110 yds.	Walk 110 yds.	4 times	4 or 5
(2)	Varied terrain and varied fartlek to cover the total day's distance.			3

Thursday Walking and stretching.

Friday
(total distance: 3¾ to 5 miles)

(1)	Jog 110 yds.	Walk 110 yds.	4 times	4 or 5
(2)	Steady fartlek for a comfortable distance.			
(3)	Jog 330-220-110 yds. Walk 110 yds. after each to complete the day's distance.			4 or 5

Saturday Optional program today or tomorrow—not both

Sunday Optional program or 30 minute walk; easy stretching

Week XII

Distance is 4 to 5 miles.

This is the last week in Plan C. Congratulations! Now what'll it be? Move ahead, stay here or drop back to something more comfortable? While you're making up your mind, test your sense of pace with a "jogger's mile" on the second day. Be sure to mark down the time on your progress chart. Review the progress chart and see how far you've come. Congratulations again.

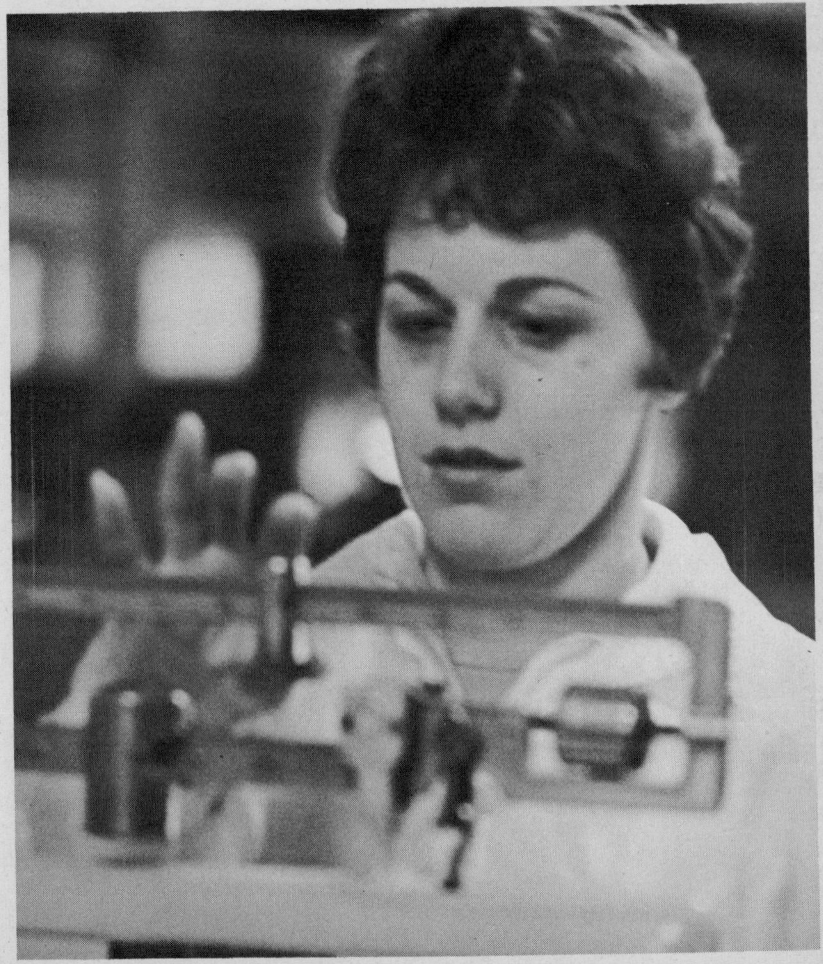

Week XII

Pace 3 = 110 yds. at 35 to 40 seconds
Pace 4 = 110 yds. at 25 to 30 seconds
Pace 5 = 110 yds. at 20 to 25 seconds

				Pace
Monday (total distance: 4 to 5 miles)				
(1)	Jog 110 yds.	Walk 110 yds.	2 times	4 or 5
(2)	Jog 880 yds.	Walk 110 yds.	2 times	4 or 5
(3)	Jog 330-220-110 yds. Walk as needed between intervals.		4 times	4 or 5
(4)	Jog 110 yds.	Walk 110 yds.	3 times	4 or 5

Tuesday Golf. Gardening. Walk.

Wednesday
(total distance: 4 to 5 miles)

(1)	Warm up 110's in preparation for a jogger's mile. You select pace.	
(2)	Jogger's mile at your selected pace.	
(3)	Slow fartlek to complete the 4 mile distance	3

Thursday Walking and stretching.

Friday
(total distance: 4 to 5 miles)

(1)	Jog 110 yds.	Walk 110 yds.	4 times	4 or 5
(2)	Varied pace fartlek.			3
(3)	Jog 110 yds. Walk 110 yds. to complete the day's distance.			4 or 5

Saturday Optional program today or tomorrow—not both

Sunday Optional program or 30 minute walk; easy stretching

13
KEEP JOGGING

For all joggers, the principal purpose of the 12-week training period is to improve your level of fitness gradually and safely so that regular moderate exercise becomes a permanent habit.

During the training period, you become aware of your needs and capacity; you also learn the proper techniques of running and become familiar with proven training methods.

The importance of avoiding over-training is emphasized.

After 12 weeks, you can see firsthand the value of better physical fitness. To stay in top shape, make a firm resolve to exercise regularly.

Here's a summary of rules to help keep you in good physical condition:

1. Train, don't strain. Never go "all-out." Avoid over-training.
2. According to your ability, follow the schedules in Plans A, B or C for a good average permanent program.
3. Avoid daily strenuous jogging. Three or four days weekly is adequate. Remember the "hard-easy" principle. Work hard one day, rest the next.
4. Jog alone or with others. And jog wherever you wish. You can always vary the scenery.
5. Remember, jogging programs are flexible. If you miss a workout or are set back for illness or other reasons, jogging lets you start again at *today's* level of fitness.

Train, don't strain. Keep it enjoyable. Jog away.

COMMUNITY JOGGING PROGRAMS

Community jogging programs are numerous. Your town or neighborhood may already have one. So, if you feel the need for professional direction before you begin to jog, by all means check around and see what's available.

FORMAL PROGRAMS

In a formal program you're looking for a professional staff with training facilities. There are some logical places to call. First, try the YMCA or YMHA; then adult education departments of either the public schools or at a college or university. Private athletic clubs and city or county parks and recreation departments are also good bets. You will have to arrange your time to meet with the group.

SEMI-FORMAL PROGRAMS

Less organized and less professional but still providing a framework around which to start a program are the service clubs, e.g. Rotary, JC's, Kiwanis. These organizations have regular meetings and officers. It is relatively easy to promote and publicize a jogging program with the help of all the membership or a subcommittee of the membership.

Church groups, chambers of commerce and local or county medical associations and heart associations are other groups that may help by sponsoring or sharing the sponsorship of a jogging program.

SPECIALIZED HELP FOR SEMI-FORMAL PROGRAMS

You semi-formal types won't have the advantages of a professional staff. Yet to make the program go, you need at least three volunteers with specialized qualifications. A medical advisor is first; second, an instructor to lead the group; and third, a public relations person (see page 123 for details of proved program).

The physician provides medical advice on aches and pains and explains the medical implications of the program. Most importantly, he detects the relatively few who should not enter any exercise program because of possible harm.

The instructor, who may be the local coach or physical education instructor, counsels on individual programs and jogs with the group, explaining the exercises before each session. Usually there are no dues and no officers. The organization provides exercise and companionship.

The public relations man, working through the various media, builds public interest in the program, handles correspondence and encourages participation.

BEWARE OF SOME INSTRUCTORS

In the formal and semi-formal programs, it is most important that the instructor understands the ideas behind jogging. Watch out for the "professional," who urges you "ever upward." This type of instructor regards you as something akin to unAmerican if you don't strive all the time. That's not what jogging is about.

You work hard during a regular day. Your aims may not be competitive, still your work is a constant attempt to achieve some goal set by you or your boss.

You should enjoy the workout by working at *your* pace.

INFORMAL PROGRAMS

Program is probably too strong a word for this activity. If you want the stimulation of running with companions, yet shun anything organized, try to get something going with the fellows in the car pool, bridge group, garden club, the neighbors or the crowd you drink with.

The only formal thing is the motto, "Train, don't strain." There are no dues. But unless you agree on a time and a place, chances are good you won't get group participation.

During the summer months you can approach the park department and ask them to set up a schedule for a weekly "jogger's mile." It creates interest and gives you a chance to meet other joggers.

Jogging is good family fun, too. Get the whole group on a regular schedule and jog together.

A PROVED PLAN FOR COMMUNITY JOGGING

If you're really interested in organizing, here is a program that has already proved itself. After reviewing the outline, you may wish to change some of the details to fit local situations.

Basic Plan

Part I—HOW TO ORGANIZE

1. Plan a 12-week program following the jogging principles outlined in this book.
2. Organize the program under the joint direction of a physician, athletic director and a public relations man who will donate their time for a community endeavor. The physician gives preliminary physical examinations and advises on various medical problems that arise during the program. The athletic director provides general over-all supervision of the actual jogging. The public relations man handles the correspondence, forms and promotion of the program.
3. Set a reasonable limitation on the number of participants: 30 to 100.
4. The organizing committee should decide upon a reasonable fee that will cover the cost of medical supplies, postage and the printing of forms. A fee also guarantees participation. Fewer drop out after coming across with hard cash. Ten to 12 dollars will be about right.
5. Enlist the support of local organizations, e.g. Chamber of Commerce or some service club. Use the organization's office as the central location to pick up and file forms and pay fees. Sometimes the organization will sponsor the program, paying the entire cost from the club treasury.
6. Encourage well known community leaders to participate. Their presence may make it "the thing to do."

Part II—BEFORE YOU BEGIN

1. The medical parts of the program are most important. There is a medical questionnaire (see page 125 for suggested form) as well as a clinical examination of the heart, lungs and blood pressure. These steps will detect the applicants who can't jog safely.

If there are doubts about the health of a prospective jogger, he should be referred to his personal physician.

2. Before starting the program, have an evening meeting of the participants. Make it the first and only formal meeting. The physician and athletic director discuss the jogging program and answer questions.

Part III—FACILITIES, TIME, ETC.

1. The use of a school or park track helps a beginning program. They permit the jogger to gauge easily how far he has traveled during a workout. When no track is available, parks, golf courses or special marked out courses in the neighborhood are suitable.

2. Men often have conflicts with business hours. Experience shows that the most convenient times for them are between 6:45 a.m. and 7:30 a.m. and between 5:00 and 5:45 p.m. Women also prefer the very early hours and early afternoons. The early morning hours bring the best attendance.

3. Lockers and shower facilities are nice but not necessary. When no special facilities are available, joggers change at home or in a car. Many prefer to come to the workouts in their jogging clothes and then shower at home.

4. During the first two weeks, the group jogs together, learning the pace and receiving coaching from the instructor. In the third week, while still maintaining group identity, joggers can jog alone, in pairs or in small groups according to ability and spontaneous preference.

5. Jogging in large groups for the full 12 weeks has its disadvantages. Joggers usually come in three broad categories of fitness. About 80 percent are moderately fit, another 10 percent are quite fit and the bottom 10 percent are relatively unfit. When mixed together, some have difficulty keeping up with the average pace while others want to jog more rapidly. Flexibility of individual schedules is necessary to sustain interest and prevent discouragement.

Part IV—(OPTIONAL)

In the Oregon programs, the joggers were divided into groups of approximately 20 and placed under the supervision of a paid staff member. The staff member usually is a high school or college rack man with knowledge of running techniques. He jogs with he participants, encourages them, keeps records of their accomplishments and adds to the companionship.

For participants in a community jogging program under the upervision of an athletic director and a physician the following orm has been useful.

PLEASE PRINT

Name ____
Last First Middle

Address ____

Occupation ______________________ Age ____________

Telephone _______________________ Date ___________

TO BE ANSWERED BY PARTICIPANT

	Yes	No
1. Have you ever had a heart attack (coronary thrombosis, myocardial infarction)? .... What hospital ______________ When _____	☐	☐
2. Have you ever been told by a doctor that you have high blood pressure, a heart murmur or heart disease?	☐	☐
3. Do you have diabetes?	☐	☐
4. Is your heart beat ever irregular, or do you have spells where it is suddenly fast?	☐	☐
5. Do you ever have chest pain on vigorous exertion?	☐	☐
6. Have you ever had lung disease?	☐	☐
7. Are you taking digitalis, quinidine, nitroglycerine or any other drug for your heart?	☐	☐
8. Are you taking any other medication prescribed by a physician at present time?	☐	☐
9. If you walked on the level for a mile at an average pace would you get out of breath, have pain in your chest, develop marked fatigue or have pains in your legs?	☐	☐
10. Do you have gout, arthritis, or rheumatism?	☐	☐
11. Do you have any disability of the feet, ankles, knees, hips or back?	☐	☐
12. Do you have a rupture or hernia?	☐	☐

13. If you are under the care of a physician, does he approve of your entering the jogging program? . . ☐ ☐
14. Do you have any illness at the present time? . . . . ☐ ☐
If "yes" describe: ______________________

____

____

15. Please list any operations or serious illnesses (except colds) that you have had in the last five years:

____

____

____

____

____

____

____

1. Medical history: negative __ significant __ reason: ________
____
____

	Start	End
2. Blood pressure	____	____
3. Pulse rate resting	____	____
4. Vital capacity	____	____

5. Immediately after exercise (Double Master Two-Step test used as standard for exercise): Pulse ______ B.P. ______ 5 minutes after exercise: Pulse ______ B.P. ______ Arrhythmia: No __ Yes __ If "yes", type ________________
6. Exercise test terminated because of dyspnea, fatigue, vertigo, chest pain, etc.: No __ Yes __ Ascent? ________________ Reason ________________________________
7. Forced expiration prolonged: No __ Yes __
8. Chest and cardiac findings normal: No __ Yes __
9. Special tests ________________________________
____
____

From tests on previous jogging programs it is concluded that an EKG, Master test, urinalysis or chest x-ray are necessary only if indicated by the history or the physical examination.

Referred to personal physician for permission to enter the program, ______, for EKG ______, for Master test ______, for chest x-ray ______, for other ________________

Accepted ______, Accepted after personal physician's permission ______, Accepted but medical observation desirable ____________.

Rejected ______ Reason ________________________

PHYSICIAN'S NOTES

____

Physician's Signature

ACKNOWLEDGMENTS

In personal success or team play, nothing is more important than that ephemeral thing, spirit. Without spirit, or whatever one wishes to call it, there would have been no jogging program, no participants and no book. Limited space and time prohibit personal "thank you's" to the great numbers who contributed to jogging through their participation and encouragement. However, special thanks are owed to Arthur Lydiard for his re-introduction to the marvelous sight of so many people jogging amidst the beauties of the New Zealand countryside; to Seymour Leiberman of Houston, Texas, for his concoction, "The Socrates Shuffle"; to Barbara Bowerman for her encouragement and for her ability to communicate the "how's" of jogging; to "Jock" Harris for his medical guidance and the unselfish giving of his own time; to Jim Shea for his editing and understanding.

WJB

The authors acknowledge the invaluable assistance of Eva Magill Abbott, Curtis Nelson, Wesley Jacobs, M.D., Helen Harris, Janet Shea and all the joggers and members of the University of Oregon track team.